Knitter's Know-How

DISCARD

Knitter's Know-How

127 Techniques Every Knitter Needs to Know

Cap Sease

Martingale®
Create with Confidence

Knitter's Know-How:
127 Techniques Every Knitter Needs to Know
© 2016 by Cap Sease

Create with Confidence

Martingale®
19021 120th Ave. NE, Ste. 102
Bothell, WA 98011-9511 USA
ShopMartingale.com

Printed in China
21 20 19 18 17 16   8 7 6 5 4 3 2 1

Library of Congress Cataloging-in-Publication Data
is available upon request.

ISBN: 978-1-60468-774-3

MISSION STATEMENT

We empower makers who use fabric and yarn to make life more enjoyable.

CREDITS

PUBLISHER AND
CHIEF VISIONARY OFFICER
Jennifer Erbe Keltner

CONTENT DIRECTOR
Karen Costello Soltys

MANAGING EDITOR
Tina Cook

ACQUISITIONS EDITOR
Karen M. Burns

TECHNICAL EDITOR
Ursula Reikes

COPY EDITOR
Marcy Heffernan

DESIGN MANAGER
Adrienne Smitke

COVER AND
INTERIOR DESIGNER
Regina Girard

PHOTOGRAPHER
Brent Kane

ILLUSTRATOR
Linda Schmidt

SPECIAL THANKS
Thanks to Molly Brusewitz
of Mad Cow Yarn in Bothell, Washington,
for providing yarn for the decorative photography .

Contents

Introduction

Finishing is all too often regarded as a necessary evil by knitters. But it's actually an integral part of the knitting process—just as important as any other step. Some might even argue it's the most important step, because how you finish a project can literally make or break it. Poor finishing will detract from an otherwise beautifully knit garment or project. Good finishing, on the other hand, enhances your work, giving it a polished and professional look.

You'll see in the first section of this book how finishing starts at the beginning of a project. While this may seem counterintuitive, thinking ahead can actually save you time and trouble, making finishing much easier. The sections that follow present the progression of steps to finishing, from weaving in ends to washing. Each gives you options so that you can choose the right technique for your particular project.

Finishing doesn't have to be difficult or time consuming. It's worth taking the time to master basic finishing techniques so that you become comfortable with them. Once that happens, you're more likely to use them. And who knows, you might even come to enjoy finishing!

Planning

Although it may sound odd, the most important part of finishing any project is planning. Before you even begin a project, you should think about the finishing. Will there be seams? Will adding selvage stitches dress up the edges or make seaming easier? Do you want both edges of your scarf to look alike? How can you have fewer ends to sew in? These are some of the decisions to make before you start that can greatly facilitate finishing and give your knitting a more professional look.

Swatches

Many knitters are so anxious to get started on a new project that they pay short shrift to the swatch. They knit a minimal swatch to check gauge and then pull it out. If you think of a swatch as a test piece, not just for checking gauge but also for testing a variety of things that will make finishing easier, you might think twice about ripping it out. This is especially true if you're using a different yarn than the one called for in your pattern.

A good-sized swatch can be used to test how a particular yarn responds to blocking and washing. The yarn label may give you recommendations about how to block or wash the yarn, but actually testing it will give you definitive information.

Here a swatch is used to determine the width of buttonholes and number of stitches for the button band as well as to try out a decorative bind off.

Your swatch can be used to try out different cast ons and bind offs or edging techniques. You can also determine the exact width for buttonholes. If you'll need to pick up stitches for neck or button bands, you can use the swatch to determine the right ratio of picked-up stitches to knit rows. So think twice before you unravel your next swatch.

Cast Ons and Bind Offs

Some edges will be finished when they come off the needles, without any further work. You want these edges to be as neat as possible so that they look good. Think about different cast-on and bind-off techniques that will give these edges the look you want. There are many options, one of which will be just right for your project.

If you want the ends of a scarf, for example, to look the same, choose a cast-on and bind-off pair that produces the same edge. If you use the common long-tail cast on, the sewn bind off makes a good match. Try the tubular cast on with the tubular bind off for matching edges. Or use a provisional cast on and knit your scarf in two directions so that the two ends are exactly the same.

Because using live stitches creates a less bulky seam, you may want to forgo binding off and keep your stitches on the needle. Or you might want to use a provisional cast on so that you can have live stitches when you're ready to make a seam or hem.

Seams

Thinking ahead about seams can make sewing knitted pieces together much easier. Knowing what you want your seams to look like will determine the best stitch to use for sewing. Do you want the seam to be invisible? Do you want the seam to be decorative and enhance the lines of your garment? Knowing which stitch produces the look you want will, in turn, tell you whether adding selvage stitches will facilitate seaming.

⟶ Seams Sew Easy ⟵

If you're knitting a project in pieces that will be joined after knitting, leave a long tail when casting on or binding off. The tail can then be used to sew the seams, leaving you with fewer ends to weave in. Make a butterfly with the tail, so it stays out of your way as you knit.

The butterflied tail will be used to sew a seam.

Selvage Stitches

Selvage stitches are added to the beginning and end of each row and are often worked in a different pattern stitch so that they stand apart from the pattern. Selvage stitches can make your edge stitches neater and more even. They can stabilize edges, especially when working in stockinette stitch, preventing them from curling. In addition, selvage stitches often facilitate sewing seams, picking up stitches, or adding embellishments such as fringes along an edge by providing a clean line that can be a guide.

Edges that will not be seams, such as scarves, are finished off the needles, so you might use selvage stitches to make these edges neat, prevent them from curling, or give them a little flair by offsetting the pattern stitch of your piece.

Selvage stitches serve as a seam allowance. They disappear into the seams and will not be visible on the finished piece, nor will they add to the width of the garment, so don't include them in your measurements if you're designing a garment.

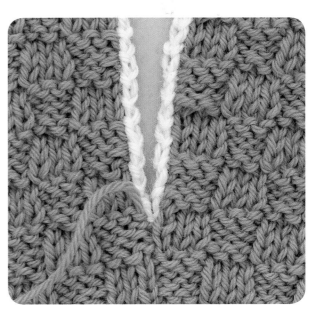

Selvage stitches in white disappear into the seam.

Selvage stitches also enable ribbing, pattern stitches, or colorwork to go all the way around your garment without being broken up by a seam. In these cases, just add an extra stitch to each end/edge of the piece that will be seamed and work it as instructed in the desired selvage. Then, use a seaming technique like mattress stitch (see page 42) that will pull the selvage stitches into the seam, making them invisible in the finished garment and letting your pattern continue uninterrupted.

White selvage stitches disappearing into the seam on K1, P1 rib

White selvage stitches disappearing into the seam on K2, P2 rib

For ribbing, add a selvage stitch to the edge that will be seamed. If both edges will be seamed, for K1, P1 rib, begin with a knit stitch and end with a purl. For K2, P2 rib, begin with P3 and end with K3. Having the selvage stitch on the left edge follow a knit stitch just to the right of the seam enables you to take advantage of the knitted texture to help hide the seam. A seam will be less noticeable if it's made after a strong vertical line (the column of knit stitches) rather than just before it.

There are many different ways to make selvage stitches, a few of which are included here.

Chain-Stitch Selvage

Also called slip-stitch selvage or open selvage

The chain-stitch selvage is the most versatile of the selvage stitches. It produces a chain along the edge of your piece with one chain stitch for every two rows. The elongated stitch makes a neat finished edge. It also makes it easy to insert a knitting needle or crochet hook under the edge stitch, so this selvage is an excellent choice when your pattern calls for picking up stitches. It's particularly useful for chunky yarns, as it cuts down on the amount of yarn along the selvage, creating less bulky seams.

Chain-stitch selvage for stockinette stitch

The chain-stitch selvage can be worked in several ways. Here are three:

Method 1

Right-side rows: Slip the first stitch knitwise with the yarn in back and knit the last stitch.

Wrong-side rows: Slip the first stitch purlwise with the yarn in front and purl the last stitch.

Method 2

Right-side rows: Knit the first stitch through the back loop and slip the last stitch knitwise with the yarn in back.

Wrong-side rows: Purl the first stitch and slip the last stitch knitwise with the yarn in back.

Method 3

All rows: Slip the first stitch purlwise with the yarn in front and knit the last stitch.

Chain-Stitch Selvage for Garter Stitch

A chain-stitch selvage makes a tidy edge on garter stitch.

All rows: Slip the first stitch purlwise with the yarn in front, and knit the last stitch through the back loop.

Chain-stitch selvage for garter stitch

Chain-Garter Selvage

The chain-garter selvage is slightly firmer than the chain-stitch selvage. It provides a good edge for picking up stitches.

Right-side rows: Slip the first stitch knitwise with the yarn in back, purl the second stitch; work to the last two stitches, purl the second to last stitch, slip the last stitch knitwise with the yarn in back.

Wrong-side rows: Purl the first two and last two stitches.

Chain-garter selvage

Stockinette-Stitch Selvage

Because it will curl, the stockinette-stitch selvage doesn't produce a good finished edge. It works well, however, for edges to be seamed, producing seams with little bulk when using the mattress stitch (see page 42).

Right-side rows: Knit the first and last stitch.

Wrong-side rows: Purl the first and last stitch.

Stockinette-stitch selvage

Garter-Stitch Selvage

Producing two edges that look slightly different, the garter-stitch selvage makes a decorative finished edge that helps prevent stockinette stitch from curling. The edge is also good for picking up stitches.

Because the edge stitch is clearly delineated, it's easy to insert a yarn needle between the first two stitches to sew a straight seam.

All rows: Knit the first and last stitch.

Garter-stitch selvage

For a good-looking finished edge (one that won't be seamed), knit the first and last two or three stitches on every row.

A wider garter-stitch selvage makes a nice edge.

Slipped Garter-Stitch Selvage

Also called beaded selvage

Use this technique for a slightly firmer edge than the garter-stitch selvage, which prevents edges from spreading or stretching. The left and right edges look slightly different.

All rows: Slip the first stitch knitwise with the yarn in back and knit the last stitch.

Slipped garter-stitch selvage

Beaded Picot Selvage

The beaded picot selvage makes a decorative edge that can be matched with the picot cast on and picot bind off. You can space the picots farther apart by working two or more rows before repeating the picot row.

All rows: Use the knit or cable cast on to cast on two stitches at the beginning of the row. Bind off the two stitches and work to the end.

Beaded picot selvage

Joining Yarn Ends

You're not alone if you hate to sew in ends after you've finished knitting. Several techniques worked during knitting can save you the trouble of facing all those ends. And they can be worked anywhere on your piece, not just at the selvage.

Most knitters recommend joining balls at the beginning or end of a row rather than making joins in the middle of a row. It's believed that ends can be hidden easily along the selvage or seam while ends woven in the middle of a row will thicken the fabric and affect its drape. Personally, I join strands whenever my ball or skein runs out. But as with most things, there are advantages and disadvantages to each method. It comes down to a matter of personal taste, and not all techniques work for all yarns. Below are some examples.

- **Lace.** It can be tricky to join in the middle when knitting open lace, unless you can change in a stockinette or garter-stitch section of the lace. Otherwise, join new yarn at the edge.

- **Scarf or shawl.** When both edges of the piece will be visible, you may find it easier to weave in ends inconspicuously in the middle rather than on the edges.
- **Chunky yarn.** Very thick yarn can add enough bulk at the join to affect the drape of the fabric, so working in the ends as you knit or joining at the edges is a better option than weaving in ends in the middle of the knitting.

Common Join

The usual method for joining yarns is to drop the old strand and begin knitting with the new one. After a row or two, the stitches on either side of the gap can be tightened up if necessary. You can either let the ends just hang or tie them in a loose knot. Then you'll need to weave in the ends later. See "Weaving in Ends" on page 18.

Hanging ends where two balls of yarn were joined

Overlapped Ends

Because the strands are knit together, overlapped ends can create a thicker section of knitting, which may or may not be visible. This technique works better with lightweight yarns. Just try it with your project yarn to see whether this is an option.

1. When you have about 4" or 5" left of the old yarn, overlap the new yarn, leaving about a 2" tail.
2. Knit three or four stitches with both strands together. Then drop the old yarn and continue knitting with the new yarn.

3. On the next row where the ends overlap, there will be two loops on the needle for each stitch. Treat each pair as one stitch and work them together. After working a few rows, trim the yarn tails to about ½". Ends don't need to be woven in. They should be sufficiently secured by the knitting together.

*Knitting old strand and
new strand loops together*

Woven Joins

With woven joins, you weave the ends in as you would secure floats in colorwork. The end is caught alternately over and under the working yarn, securing it to the back of your knitting.

1. Drop the old yarn, leaving a 5" tail. Leaving a similar length tail on the new yarn, knit the next stitch, bringing the working yarn under the old end.

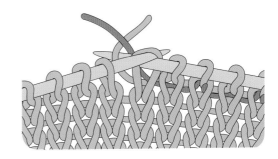

2. Knit the next stitch, bringing the working yarn over the old end.

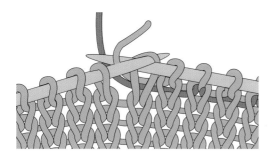

3. Repeat steps 1 and 2 for about eight stitches, then trim both ends (the old and new yarn tails).

4. You can weave in the ends in the same manner on a purl row.

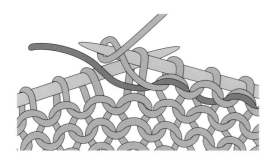

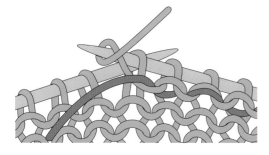

Spit Splice

Also called spit splicing or spit and splice

An easy technique that produces an invisible join, the spit splice can be made anywhere in a row. It works especially well with wool and wool blends, as the little barbs on wool help to make the fibers stick together. It's also useful for lace and reversible projects, such as scarves, where you don't want to weave in ends along the edges.

When the end of the old yarn is about 8" long, separate the plies. With two-ply yarn, break off about 2" to 3" of one ply. With three-ply (or more) yarn, break off each ply in a different place. Don't cut the plies, as you want a loose, tapered end. A blunt end won't splice neatly. Gently pull apart the fibers on the remaining ply so that the end is open and fluffy. Repeat this on the end of the new yarn.

Separate plies and fluff them prior to splicing.

Overlap the tapered ends on the palm of your hand with the strands going in opposite directions. Lick the other palm and quickly roll the ends between your palms until the strands stick together, about 5 to 10 seconds. If you're averse to spit, use a damp paper towel or sponge to moisten your palm.

Overlap ends on palm, ready for splicing.

Splice singles in the same way by untwisting each end and picking the fibers apart. Then, holding the yarn firmly between two fingers, gently pull the fibers out to taper the ends before splicing.

Russian Join

A Russian join is quite strong, but the overlap will be a bit thicker than the yarn. It's especially useful in lace knitting.

1. Loop the two ends around each other; then thread one end onto a tapestry needle.
2. Thread the yarn back into the center of itself for about 1" and pull the end through. Repeat with the other end.

Insert the needle into the center of the strand.

3. Holding the ends, pull the strands apart gently to tighten and straighten the join, then cut the tails.

Pull strands apart to tighten the join.

Magic-Knot Join

Two knots are used to make this join. It creates a strong join, but the knots will probably be felt, depending on your yarn. It may not be possible to hide the trimmed ends. If you don't like knots in knitting, this join is not for you.

1. Place the old and new ends parallel to each other on a flat surface so that they overlap about 5" or 6", with the ends on opposite sides.

Lay out two ends for a magic-knot join.

2. Bring the new end under the old strand, then back over it and the new strand to make a loop around the old strand. Bring the new end up into the loop from underneath to make a knot with the new yarn around the old strand.

Loop and knot the new end around the old end.

3. Repeat step 2 with the old end to make a knot around the new strand.

Repeat, so both ends are knotted around each other.

4. Pull each knot tight, then gently pull both strands away from each other to pull the two knots together. Trim the ends.

Pull strands away from each other to tighten the join.

Shaping

How you shape your garment can facilitate seaming. For example, if you work increases and decreases a stitch or two inside the selvage, the edge stitch remains unchanged, creating a smooth edge that will make sewing easier.

Work decreases two stitches in from the edge for easier seaming.

If your pattern calls for shaping over several rows, at the shoulder, for example, consider working short rows rather than groups of stepped bind offs. Short rows enable you to increase rows in some areas without binding off in others, making straighter, neater edges that will be easier to sew.

Work short-row shaping, as shown along the top-right edge, to make a smooth edge that's easier to sew than the stepped edges on the left, created by binding off the stitches.

To work short rows, work to the turning point as specified in the pattern.

1. Slip the next stitch purlwise and bring the yarn to the opposite side between the needles. If it's in the back, bring it to the front. If it's in the front, bring it to the back.

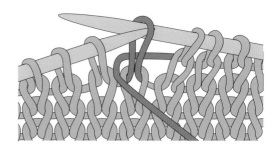

2. Slip the stitch back to the left needle and move the yarn to the opposite side into position for the next stitch. This will wrap the working strand around the slipped stitch. Turn work. Steps 1 and 2 are called wrap and turn, or W&T.

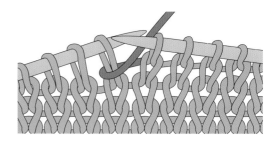

3. Work short rows the same way on purl rows.

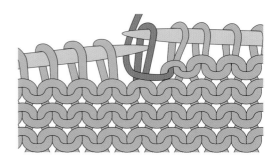

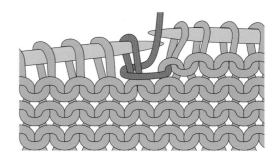

When all the short rows are completed, hide the wraps so that they don't show on the front. If you're going to bind off immediately, you may be able to skip this last step. You can also skip it if working in garter stitch.

After the last wrap and turn, on a knit row, work across all the stitches in the row. When you reach a wrapped stitch, insert the right needle under the front strand of the wrap, then into the stitch and knit the two together.

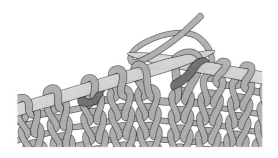

To hide the wraps on a purl row, work to the wrapped stitch. Pick up the wrap with the right needle, slip it onto the left needle, and purl it together with the stitch.

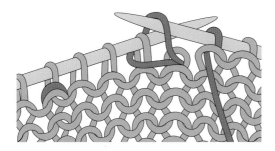

On the fronts of garments, the wrap and turns will be made on the outside of each shoulder. On the back, wrap and turn on both shoulder edges.

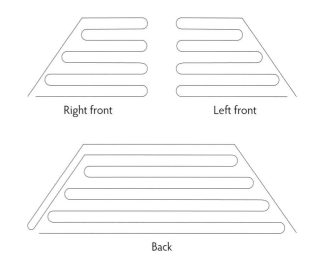

Right front   Left front

Back

⟿ Seaming Short-Row ⟿ Shoulders

After working short-row shaping on shoulders, use the three-needle bind off (see page 36) to give you a smooth, even seam.

Weaving in Ends

Ends are the tails left hanging where you joined a new ball of yarn during knitting. Weaving, sewing, or darning in ends is the way to handle loose ends to prevent your knitting from unraveling. If you haven't worked in the ends as you knit your project, you'll have to secure them as part of finishing. See "Joining Yarn Ends" on page 12.

Nothing makes a handknit garment look more amateurish than yarn ends that have pulled out, leaving little stubs sticking up. So make sure you weave ends in far enough that they don't pull out. For most wool or wool blends, 1" is sufficient. With wear, wool yarns tend to mat together a bit, which will help keep them from pulling out. Cotton and some synthetic yarns can be quite slippery and are more likely to pull out, unless you weave them in for more than 1". Some knitters recommend separating the plies on slippery yarns and weaving them in separately. While this does help to secure the ends, it means there are twice as many ends to work in. Also, don't trim ends too short. After weaving them in, stretch the fabric before trimming the ends. This will help ensure you leave long enough ends. Then trim the ends, leaving about ½".

A short end pulled out onto the right side is unsightly.

Especially slippery yarns may need to be tied together before weaving in to keep them from slipping. Although many knitters do not like knots anywhere in their work, I feel they sometimes have a place in knitting, and this is one of them. If the knot is quite tight, it should not affect the look of your project.

Yarn needle or tapestry needle? A yarn needle is large with a big eye and blunt point. It's good for sewing seams; you can easily go around stitches rather than through them. It's also best with thick yarn. A tapestry needle is smaller, with a sharper point than a yarn needle. The sharper point makes a tapestry needle good for weaving in ends. Because it's smaller, it works well with fine yarns. Keep both on hand and use whichever works best for your purpose.

Weaving in at Edges

If you tied the two strands together to secure them during knitting, untie the knot. Check to make sure the stitches at the join on the front are the right size. Sometimes they become smaller if the knot is pulled too tight. Adjust the size of the stitches if necessary.

Twist the two ends around each other to close the gap in the knitting. Thread one end onto the tapestry needle and work it through the selvage stitches for at least 1" before cutting it. I like to sew the end around the sides of the selvage stitches working up or down a column of stitches as shown at the top of page 19. The end is less visible and the more the end weaves around the project yarn, the more secure it will be. Repeat with the other end, working it in the opposite direction.

Ends woven around the sides of selvage stitches (top) and in through selvage stitches (bottom). White yarn was used for clarity.

If your pieces will be seamed, it's best to weave in the ends after sewing the seams. Ends worked along the selvage stitches can make it more difficult to make neat, even seams. Once the seams are sewn, weave the ends through the seam. I find a zigzag pattern along the seam works well.

Zigzag the ends through the seam. White yarn was used for clarity.

Weaving in Mid-Row

Sometimes joining two yarns in the middle of a row is unavoidable. In circular knitting, for example, you won't have selvages or seams so you'll have to join yarns in the middle. Some color techniques, such as intarsia, will also require mid-row joins. Some knitters feel that weaving in ends in the middle thickens the fabric and shows on the front. I don't find this to be the case as long as the woven-in ends match the tension of the knitting.

If you tied the two ends together during knitting, undo the knots and adjust the size of the stitches at the join if necessary. Twist the two ends around each other and thread one onto a tapestry needle. You have several options to work in the ends.

Horizontal Weaving

You can weave the end in horizontally through the tops of a row of stitches. Insert the threaded needle from above under the top of each stitch as you work along the row for at least 1" to secure the end. Or zigzag in and out of each stitch along a row alternately from above and below; then trim the end. If the yarn is slippery and you're not sure it's secure, work back the other way through the tops of stitches a row above or below for about half the distance.

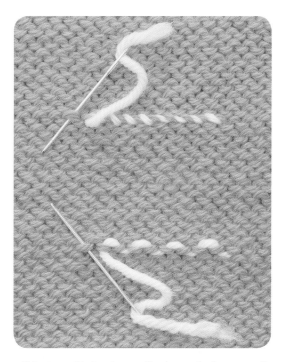

Weave ends horizontally through the tops of stitches (top) or zigzag in and out of stitches (bottom). White yarn was used for clarity.

Vertical Weaving

You can also weave ends in vertically up or down a column of stitches, but it must be done very carefully, or the ends will show on the right side of the garment. Vertical weaving works best with ribbing, wrapping the end around the sides of a column of stitches.

Weave end vertically up the sides of a column of stitches of ribbing. White yarn was used for clarity.

Duplicate Stitch

I prefer to use the purl duplicate stitch, as I find the end is more secure. Because the end winds up and down along the row, it's less likely to pull out. Duplicate stitch is particularly good with reversible projects.

Duplicate stitch is worked on the right side of stockinette stitch. You can work toward the right or the left.

End woven in with duplicate stitch. White yarn was used for clarity.

1. Thread one yarn end into a yarn needle and then insert the needle up through the center of the V below the one you want to cover, then insert it under both loops of the stitch above.

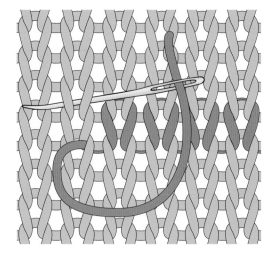

2. Insert the needle back through the same stitch where you came out.

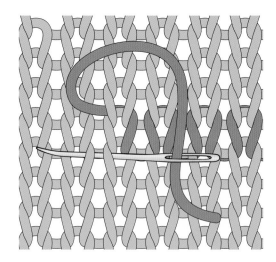

Reverse the process for the other end.

⚊ *Duplicate Stitch in Pattern* ⚊

Work the duplicate stitch on a pattern stitch using a combination of both versions of the stitch. Look carefully at the strand of yarn you want to follow; then use your needle to work a knit or a purl duplicate of the stitch to weave the end in.

Purl Duplicate Stitch

The purl version of the duplicate stitch is worked on the reverse of stockinette stitch.

End woven in with purl duplicate stitch. White yarn was used for clarity.

1. Twist the two yarn ends around each other.
2. Thread one yarn end into a yarn needle and insert the threaded needle up under the top of the same stitch the end came from. Following the path of the end, insert the needle up under the running strand between the stitch above and the stitch to its left, and pull the yarn through.

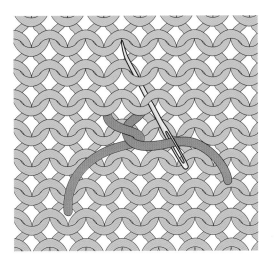

3. Insert the needle down under the running strand between the stitch above and the stitch to its right, then down under the top of the stitch you started with, and pull the yarn through.

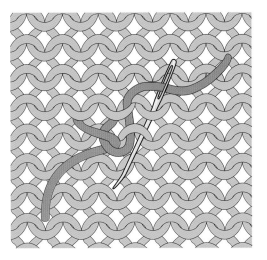

4. Move over one stitch to the right and repeat steps 2 and 3, making sure to mimic the tension of your knitting.

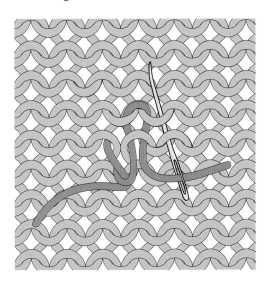

Reverse the process for the other end, working to the left.

Weaving in Ends
on Circular Knitting

Usually there's a pronounced jog between the first and last bound-off stitches in circular knitting. You can minimize this when sewing in the tail.

1. Bind off until one stitch remains on the right needle. Break the yarn and pull the knitting needle up to pull the end through the last stitch.

2. Thread the tail onto a yarn needle. Insert the needle under both sides of the first bound-off stitch and pull the yarn through.

Weave tail through the first bound-off stitch.

3. Insert the yarn needle into the center of the last bound-off stitch where the tail came out. Pull the yarn through and tighten the loop to match the tension of the bound-off stitches. The loop will look like another bound-off stitch.

Weave tail back through the last bound-off stitch.

4. Weave the end in along the inside of your piece, referring to the previously described methods. You can see the benefit of using the invisible join in the following photos.

Jog at end of circular bind off

Invisible join at end of circular bind off

Weaving in Ends on Intarsia

With intarsia, you end up with many ends on the back of your work. These ends can be woven in like any other mid-row ends. The only trick is to not mix colors. Thread the tails onto a tapestry needle. Weave the ends in behind stitches of the same color or along the edges between two colors. When knitting intarsia, make sure you leave ends long enough so that you can weave them in easily.

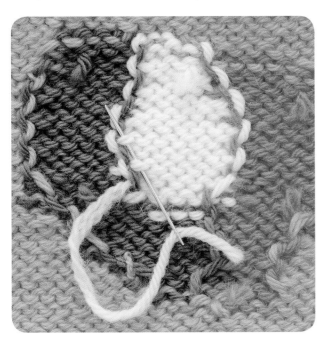

Weaving in ends on intarsia

Weaving in Intarsia Ends

If you find that the stitch on the right side where the end finished is pulled out of shape when weaving in the end, make sure you weave the end first in the direction it would have continued in if knitted. For example, if the strand was being worked on a right side before being dropped, start weaving it in on the wrong side, working to the right.

Weaving in Short Ends

If you find you have very short ends, you can still weave them in securely, although doing so can be tedious.

1. Starting where the end comes out, insert the needle along the back of a row of stitches or up a column of stitches until the eye of the needle is close to the yarn end.

2. Thread the end onto the needle and pull the needle through.

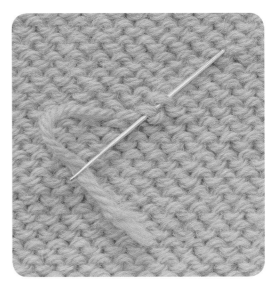

Short ends on wrong side

You may find that you have to repeat this process several times to work in the end.

Blocking

Blocking involves wetting or steaming a knit piece to flatten and shape it, and possibly to finish the surface. Once considered an essential part of finishing, it's less prevalent these days. I find that in many instances knitting really doesn't require blocking. Some unevenness provides a liveliness unique to hand knitting, and you don't want to remove it with heavy blocking.

Some knitters mistakenly feel that blocking will ensure that their garment will fit. If you've knit consistently to gauge, blocking shouldn't be required to achieve the right fit. At best, blocking allows only minor tweaks to size and shape. The extent to which this can be done will depend largely on your yarn and gauge. Some fibers are more resilient than others and will respond better to blocking than others. Similarly, a looser gauge will allow for more movement of the yarn than a tighter one. Just bear in mind that any gain in width will result in a loss in length and vice versa.

Blocking can take the life out of some fibers, flattening and compressing them so that they lose their resiliency and bounce. Textured and novelty yarns, such as bouclé or chenille, can be permanently flattened and damaged by some blocking techniques. Textured and raised stitches can also be flattened and lose their definition with injudicious blocking. Aran patterns, for example, must be blocked carefully, if at all, to ensure the cables and textured stitches show to advantage.

And contrary to common belief, there's nothing permanent about blocking. Any changes imparted to your knitting through blocking will last only until the next washing. Having said this, blocking does have its uses. It can flatten the curl on stockinette-stitch edges prior to sewing, greatly facilitating sewing seams. A judicious use of blocking can also help to flatten edgings and bands, allowing them to lie flat and fit better.

Unblocked colorwork

Colorwork after blocking

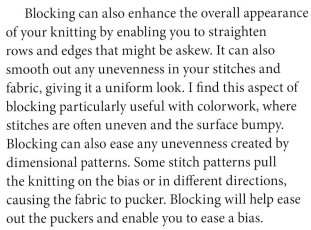

Unblocked lace

Lace after blocking

Blocking can also enhance the overall appearance of your knitting by enabling you to straighten rows and edges that might be askew. It can also smooth out any unevenness in your stitches and fabric, giving it a uniform look. I find this aspect of blocking particularly useful with colorwork, where stitches are often uneven and the surface bumpy. Blocking can also ease any unevenness created by dimensional patterns. Some stitch patterns pull the knitting on the bias or in different directions, causing the fabric to pucker. Blocking will help ease out the puckers and enable you to ease a bias.

Blocking is essential with lace knitting. Lace has a tendency to pull together or collapse in on itself as it's worked. Blocking enables you to open up the stitches to see the intricacies of the lace pattern. It also helps accentuate details like picots and scalloped edges.

If your pieces will be sewn together, it's generally best to block them first. This will make sewing seams much easier, and it's difficult to block a garment once it's been sewn together. On the other hand, some fibers, like cotton, can shrink during blocking, so it might be better to assemble a cotton garment first to help control the shrinkage and shape.

There are two basic ways to block knitting, wet blocking and steam blocking. The result is the same for both, but both methods aren't suitable for all fibers. For more on this, refer to "Wet Blocking" on page 27 and "Steam Blocking" on page 28.

Before Blocking

Blocking is not suitable for all yarns, so make sure that the fibers in your yarn can withstand the process. Wool is quite resilient and can be blocked. Cotton and linen are less resilient and, although they can be blocked, they won't respond as readily as wool. Mohair and angora cannot always be blocked successfully. Their long fibers can mat and even felt from the application of moisture and heat. Synthetics, too, can be problematic. Some can withstand blocking while others can't. Many are heat sensitive, so steaming may not be advisable. Check the yarn label for important information about the care of the fiber. See "Washing" on page 105. In general, if a yarn is washable, it can also be wet blocked. Novelty yarns, as a general rule, shouldn't be blocked. If you have any doubts, err on the side of caution and have the piece dry cleaned.

Since blocking involves water, check to make sure your yarn is colorfast, especially if more than one color is involved. Most commercial yarns are colorfast, but if they were hand dyed or painted, there may be residual dye left in the fibers. To test for colorfastness, immerse a piece of the yarn in cool water. Then wrap it around a white paper towel. If there is any color transfer to the towel, don't block your piece. Have it dry cleaned instead.

Color has transferred to the towel, indicating the yarn is not colorfast.

Prepare a proper surface on which to lay out your pieces. Choose a flat surface that is large enough to easily accommodate the entire piece, or pieces. It should also be in an out-of-the-way place as your piece will need to remain flat until it has dried completely.

Pad the surface, especially if you plan to use pins. Special blocking mats are ideal for this, but you can also make your own surface. Several towels over a wooden board or piece of foam work well. Some people use beds, pinning directly into the mattress that has been covered with a sheet of plastic. An ironing board can work well for smaller pieces.

A number of special tools are available that are designed purposely for blocking specific knitted garments. They include shawl frames, sock forms, woolly boards, hat molds, and wires for blocking lace.

Laying Out

The laying out and pinning process is common to all methods of blocking.

You can block knitting either face up or face down. Both ways have advantages and disadvantages. Face up gives you more control over the process as you can see what is happening on the right side. And you can easily manipulate cables, bobbles, and raised stitches with your fingers to ensure that they remain raised. Blocking face down protects the right side of your knitting, preventing the stitches from becoming

too flat. It will also prevent an iron from burnishing some yarns and fibers, giving them an unpleasant sheen. Use your swatch to test which method works best for your yarn.

Whether face up or down, the laying-out process is the same. Spread out the piece, being careful not to pull or stretch it too much. Overstretching will distort the dimensions of your piece as well as your stitches. If a piece is pulled too much horizontally, it will lose length; if pulled too much vertically, it will lose width.

Place the knitted piece on a blocking surface.

Start in the middle and use your hands to carefully smooth the knitting, working out toward the sides. Never pull the knitting. Gently lift and move it in small increments to reach the right place. Use a tape measure to ensure that the piece conforms to the measurements of your pattern. Once the piece is laid out, you can make minor adjustments. For example, make sure the seams are straight and that the sides of a garment match. Be very careful not to stretch ribbing, or it can lose its resiliency.

Laying out dry pieces requires pinning to keep them in position. As you lay them out, pin strategic points, for example the outside corners of the underarm and the shoulders, to the measurements of your pattern. Once the basic shape has been pinned, place pins between the already positioned pins. If the pins create points along the knitted edge, you have pulled the knitting too much. Reposition the pins so that the edge is straight.

Pin the piece to the correct dimensions.

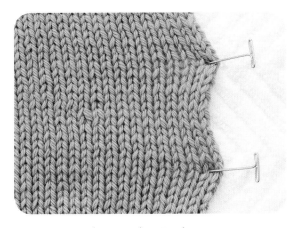

Make sure the pins have not pulled the edge out of shape, as shown here.

If you use pins, make sure they're stainless steel. You don't want rust stains on your knitting. Stainless steel T-pins work extremely well for blocking. Available in different lengths, they're strong and easy to use, and the T-top keeps the pins from getting lost in the knitted fabric. Dressmaker's pins are not a good choice. Thinner than T-pins, they are more likely to bend under pressure, and their small, round head can become lost in the knitting.

Wet Blocking

You can do wet blocking in three different ways. Each is equally effective, and it depends on your yarn and the desired look you want as to which is the best choice. Just remember that protein fibers, such as wool, alpaca, and cashmere, lose strength when wet. Without careful handling, they can stretch and become damaged.

Spraying

Spray blocking is the mildest form of wet blocking and gives you the most control. It's good for light blocking of all fibers.

Lay out your dry knitting on a prepared surface. Using a sprayer, or mister, lightly spray the surface until it's damp. Use your hands to gently press the moisture into the knitting. Allow the knitting to dry thoroughly before moving it.

Wet Towel

The wet-towel, or damp-finishing, method involves a little more moisture that goes deeper into the fibers. This method is good for all fibers, especially cotton, acrylic, fluffy, and synthetic yarns. It's also good with textured stitches.

Thoroughly soak a large bath towel in water. Then spin it in your washing machine or wring it to remove the excess water. The amount of moisture removed depends on the degree of blocking you desire. Use a wetter towel for heavy blocking or a damp one for lighter blocking.

For heavier blocking, spread out the towel and lay out your dry knitting on it. Roll them up together and leave them for at least an hour or until the knitting absorbs the moisture and is damp. Unwrap the knitting and lay it out on a flat surface to dry, pinned to shape, if necessary.

For lighter blocking, lay out your knitting to the correct dimensions on a flat surface and place the damp towel on top of it. Press the towel with your hands gently but firmly so it is in contact with the surface of the knitting. Keep the towel in place until the knitting is thoroughly dry.

Immersion

Immersion is the most vigorous form of wet blocking, as water thoroughly permeates the fiber. For obvious reasons, it can be combined with washing. It enables you to reshape pieces and change dimensions somewhat. It's good for most fibers and especially for heavily textured fabrics and lace.

Completely immerse your piece in lukewarm water until the fibers are saturated, usually about 20 minutes. Drain the water off and gently squeeze the water out of your knitting. Never wring out a piece of knitting, as this will distort the stitches and can cause felting. Spread the knitting out on a large, clean towel. Roll the two up together and squeeze the roll gently to pull more water out of the knitting.

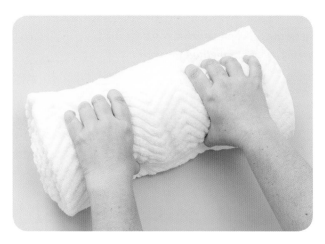

Roll the wet knitting in a towel and squeeze the towel to draw much of the moisture out of the fibers.

You can also spin out excess moisture in your washing machine. This is an effective way to remove a great deal of moisture so that the knitting dries fairly quickly. Set the dial to spin and allow it to spin for only 10 to 15 seconds.

Lay out the damp knitting on a prepared flat surface and allow it to dry before moving it.

Steam Blocking

Steam blocking requires a steam iron or a steamer to saturate the knitting with moisture and heat. Not all fibers can withstand steam, so check your yarn label before steam blocking. See "Washing" on page 105. If the label isn't specific, you can test whether or not a yarn can take steaming. Wrap a length of yarn around your fingers several times to make a coil. If you want, you can tie the coil to make a butterfly. Steam the coil. If it remains limp when dry, don't use steam.

Two yarns tested for withstanding steaming. The one on the right didn't bounce back as the one on the left did.

Lay out your dry knitting on a prepared surface. Set the iron or steamer to as low a temperature setting as possible while still producing steam. High temperatures can ruin some synthetic fibers. Pass the iron or steamer about 1" or so above the surface of your knitting. Don't touch the surface with the iron. Direct contact can cause scorching and can make the surface of some fibers shiny.

For very gentle blocking, you can quickly spritz your knitting with steam, and then pat it with your hands to even and flatten the surface.

An alternative, less harsh method is to use a pressing cloth. Place a dry cloth, such as a dish towel, on top of your knitting, then gently apply the steam iron to the cloth. The cloth moderates the heat and steam. Or you can use a damp cloth with a dry iron.

 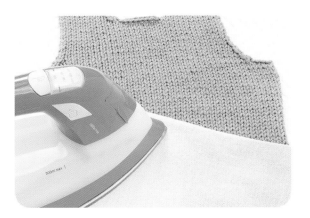

Always hold the steam iron at least 1" above the knitting.

For fibers requiring gentle blocking, apply steam through a pressing cloth.

Recommended Blocking Methods

The following table is only a guide. Check the label on your yarn for specific information. To determine the best blocking method for your yarn, test your swatch.

Wool, wool blends	Wet block or steam
Merino	Wet spray
Alpaca	Wet spray
Cashmere	Wet spray
Mohair	Wet spray
Silk	Wet spray or light steam low heat
Cotton, cotton blends	Steam
Linen	Wet block or steam
Lyocell, rayon, viscose	Wet block
Bamboo	Wet block
Soy	Wet block
Acrylics	Light steam
Synthetics	Usually wet spray, check label
Novelties	Don't block, check label

Seam Basics

Seams are generally not the most enjoyable part of a project. Knitters like to knit and often regard sewing as a tedious chore. As a result, seams are more often than not an afterthought, just something one does to assemble a project in a rush at the end. Some knitters avoid them at all costs, using circular needles to make seamless, or almost-seamless, garments. Circular knitting certainly has its place, but it isn't suited to all projects or to all knitting techniques.

Seams do have advantages, and it can be worth the time and patience required to make a good one. Knit fabric is inherently stretchy, so over time knitted garments can stretch and lose their shape. Because sewn seams are firm, they prevent stretch and provide structure to a garment. This is particularly important for shoulder seams, since they bear the weight of the entire sweater. Without a strong seam, shoulders will stretch, which in turn can pull the rest of the garment out of shape. For this reason, larger-sized or unusually long garments benefit from being seamed.

Some yarns, while beautiful and nicely draping, are limp and don't have as much substance or body as others. Garments made from these yarns can benefit from side seams to help give them definition and shape, making all the difference in the final appearance of your garment and the way it fits and wears.

Other yarns, such as over-twisted single plies, energized singles, and chenilles, have a strong bias that can usually be controlled with firm seams. Similarly, garments knit with heavyweight or bulky yarns can also benefit from seams to support the weight.

In the end, there's a time and a place for all joining techniques in knitting. Your choice of whether or not to have a seam will depend on your preference, pattern, and choice of yarn.

Requirements for Seams

No matter which technique you use to make a seam, there are some general requirements for all seams.

Most seams should be unobtrusive. They don't have to be invisible, but they shouldn't detract from your knitting. They shouldn't be the focal point of your work unless you want them to be a design element. Some seams can be decorative as well as functional, and you can use them to dress up or add a flourish to your piece.

Seams should be flat and smooth, with as little bulk as possible. Minimal, flat seams will also make some garments more comfortable to wear, especially socks.

Seams should be elastic, in keeping with the knitted fabric and with the seam's place in a garment. Too tight or rigid a seam, for example around an armhole, will restrict the movement of the garment, while one that is too loose will be sloppy and allow the fabric to stretch, especially along the shoulders. Similarly, tight or loose seams can affect the drape of afghans, blankets, and other flat pieces.

Seams should be straight. This is especially important for seams that are integral to the design of a piece—for example, the seams between raglan sleeves and the sweater body, in modular knitting, or between pieces in an afghan.

Patterns should align. The pieces being joined should match accurately to ensure that the seams lie flat and don't pucker. The rows on one piece should line up with the corresponding rows on the other. This is especially important if you have a horizontal pattern stitch or colorwork. Columns of stitches should also be aligned—for example, with ribbing or other vertical patterns.

Before Assembly

If you plan to block your knitting, do so before any assembly takes place. If working with cotton, you may want to assemble your piece first to help control shrinking. It's easier to block pieces when they're flat, and blocked pieces will make it easier to make neat seams. Even if you don't usually block your knitting, you may find a gentle pressing of the edges to be sewn will facilitate seaming.

Unless a pattern calls for a certain sequence, there is a generally established sequence for assembling most garments. The shoulder seams are joined first, as they are the foundation of a sweater. Then the sleeves are sewn to the body, followed by the side and underarm seams. Following are examples of various sweater types and the order in which the pieces are sewn together.

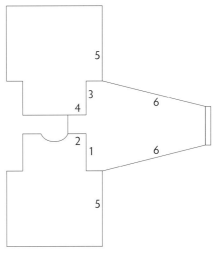

Saddle Shoulder.
Numbers indicate sewing order.

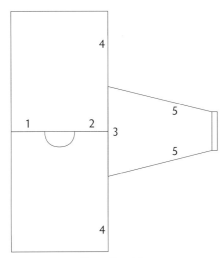

Drop Shoulder.
Numbers indicate sewing order.

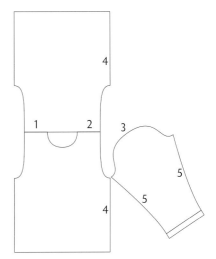

Cap (Set-in) Sleeve.
Numbers indicate sewing order.

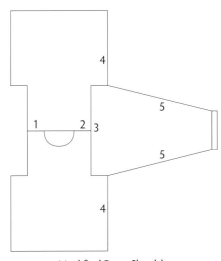

Modified Drop Shoulder.
Numbers indicate sewing order.

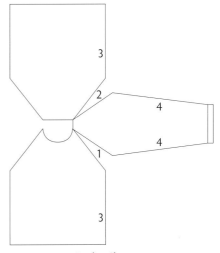

Raglan Sleeve.
Numbers indicate sewing order.

Sewing Seams on Right or Wrong Side

Seams can be worked on either the right or wrong side. The advantage of working on the right side is that you can see what you're doing, so it's easier to make straight seams. It's also recommended for colorwork and many pattern stitches where alignment of the two pieces is critical. Many knitters sew (or crochet or knit) seams from the wrong side and can produce neat seams. If you're more comfortable doing this, there's nothing wrong with it. Sewn seams worked from the wrong side tend to be a bit more straightforward and easier to work. Try both ways and see what works best for you. See "Sewn Seams" on page 39.

Some seams can be worked from either side, producing a different effect each way; one example is the three-needle bind off (see page 36).

Pinning

For most seams, it's a good idea to pin the pieces to be joined before starting to sew in order to prevent the pieces from moving as you work. Dressmaker's pins are not generally satisfactory for knitting. They are too short to securely hold most yarn thicknesses and, being made of steel, they don't grip the yarn and will easily slip out. Marking pins, because they are longer and have big heads and rounded points, work well. Bamboo or plastic pins specifically made for use with yarn work extremely well, as do coil-less safety pins and some stitch markers.

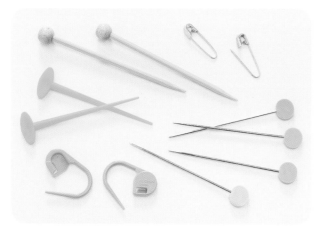

A variety of pins are available for use with knitting.

Seams worked on the wrong side generally require more pinning than those worked on the right side. Don't be stingy with pins if you want a professional-looking seam.

Using many pins will keep your pieces from moving when sewing on the wrong side.

When working seams on the right side, for example with the mattress stitch or some of the edge-to-edge stitches, pinning is less critical, as the seam is usually worked stitch by stitch or row by row. You may find it helpful, though, to use a few pins or locking markers to loosely hold the pieces in position as you sew.

Locking markers are helpful when sewing on the right side.

Direction of Seams

Generally it doesn't matter in which direction you work a seam. If it does matter, the project instructions will give you specific directions. Otherwise, consider the seam. Is there an edge that needs to be even—for example, the cuff or hem or neck edge of a raglan sleeve? If so, start there and work toward the underarm, where it won't matter if the pieces don't match exactly.

Reinforcing Seams

If you're concerned that a sewn seam will stretch, you can reinforce it with a row of slip-stitch crochet (see page 34). When using this stitch to reinforce a seam, use a hook two sizes smaller than the project needles and be sure to work through both layers of the seam.

A row of slip-stitch crochet can reinforce a seam and prevent it from stretching. White yarn was used for clarity.

⟶ *Machine Stitching* ⟵

I don't recommend machine sewing for seaming knitted projects. The machine stitches and thread are tight and not in keeping with the loft and drape of the knitted fabric. Even the longest machine stitches will be too tight and create a deep channel along the seam.

Compared to other fabrics, knitting is slippery and doesn't feed evenly under the machine's presser foot. This makes it extremely difficult to make neat seams or place them exactly where you want them. Having said this, machine stitching is useful for securing the cut edges of steeks (see page 71). The rows of machine stitches won't show, and the tight stitches will firmly secure the edges.

Crocheted Seams

Crocheted seams tend to be less elastic than knitted or sewn ones. The seam is sturdy and a bit thicker and bulkier than others. You can counteract this bulk by using a thinner yarn of the same color. Crocheted seams are generally worked from the wrong side and can be worked on selvages and cast-on or bound-off edges. They're particularly good with fragile or heavily textured novelty yarns, as only a small amount of yarn is pulled through at any one time, giving less opportunity for it to fray or pull apart. Crocheted seams are easy to rip out if you make a mistake or want to recycle the yarn.

Slip-Stitch Crochet

Also called crochet chain stitch, single crochet, crocheted seam, slip stitch

Slip-stitch crochet creates a seam that is sturdy and even, but thick. It can be worked with bound-off edges, for example on shoulder seams or with selvages on side seams.

If you want a quick, temporary seam to check the fit or shaping of a garment, this is a good stitch to use. To take out the seam, simply pull the end to unzip the seam.

Slip-stitch crochet seam worked on a stockinette-stitch garment side seam.

When using this stitch to join bound-off edges, it helps to have used a bind off that produces a chain along the edge, such as the standard bind off or the decrease bind off. When using it to join side seams, be sure you have worked chain-stitch selvages on both pieces. See "Chain-Stitch Selvage" on page 10.

Although this stitch can be worked any distance from the edge, it's best worked under the edge stitches. The farther it's worked from the edge, the bulkier the seam will be.

1. Place the pieces with right sides together. Make a slipknot and place it on the hook.

2. Insert the hook under the selvage chain stitch (or the edge stitch) of each piece, catch the yarn, and pull the yarn through the fabric and the loop on the hook.

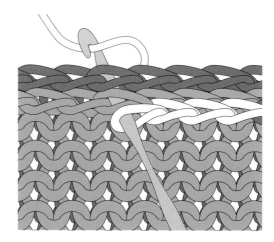

3. Insert the hook under the next pair of stitches to the left and pull a loop through both stitches and then through the loop on the hook.

4. Repeat step 3 to the end of the seam.

Two-Needle Crochet

Similar to the three-needle bind off (page 36), two-needle crochet is worked with a crochet hook instead of a third needle. It produces a strong seam that is particularly good for shoulder seams.

Two-needle crochet seam worked on a stockinette-stitch shoulder seam.

1. With the two pieces to be joined still on the needles, place them with right sides together and the needles parallel and pointing to the right.

2. Insert the hook knitwise into the first stitch on each needle and slip the stitches off the needles. Catch the yarn and pull it through both loops on the hook.

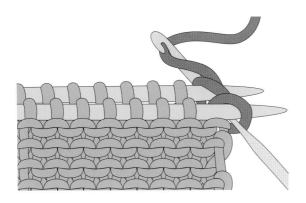

3. Insert the hook into the next stitch on each needle and slip the stitches off the needles. Catch the yarn and pull it through all three loops on the hook.

4. Repeat step 3 to the end of the seam.

Single Crochet

Single-crochet seams are worked on the right side, creating a decorative ridge along the seam on selvages or bound-off edges.

Single-crochet seam worked as a shoulder seam outside of the garment.

1. With wrong sides together, insert the hook under the inner sides of both edge stitches. Catch the yarn and pull it through. Repeat through the next pair of edge stitches to the left.

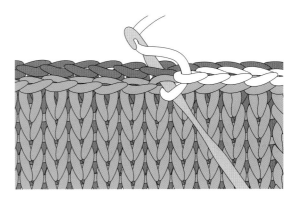

2. Catch the yarn and pull it through both loops on the hook.

3. Insert the hook under the inner sides of the next pair of edge stitches to the left. Catch the yarn and pull it through. Catch the yarn again and pull it through both stitches on the hook.

4. Repeat step 3 to the end of the seam.

Knitted Seams

The major advantage of knitted seams is that they are most in keeping with the nature of the knitted fabric. Use the same materials and tools that you used in creating the garment, and the seam will be resilient and elastic. The techniques for knitting seams are actually bind offs, but because they create a seam, I included a few of the more useful ones below.

Three-Needle Bind Off

Also called knitted bind off, bind-off seam, joinery bind off

The three-needle bind off lets you join two pieces as they are bound off. It creates a neat, strong seam that is especially good for shoulders, because it will prevent shoulders from stretching. When used with short-row shaping, it creates a particularly attractive seam.

If the right sides face each other when working the bind off, the seam will be on the inside of the garment. If the wrong sides face each other, the seam will create a decorative ridge on the right side. The two sides of the ridge are different, so if it's important to make them look alike, for example on the shoulders, work one shoulder seam from right to left and the other from left to right.

Three-needle bind off, worked right sides together

Three-needle bind off, worked wrong sides together

You'll need three needles for this technique, and the extra one should be the same size as the ones you've knit with.

1. With the two pieces of knitting to be joined still on the needles, place them with their right sides (or wrong sides) together and the needles parallel and pointing toward the right. Insert a third needle into the first stitch on each needle and knit the two stitches together using one of the working strands.

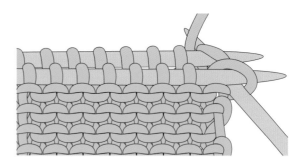

2. Knit the next stitch on each needle as in step 1.
3. With one of the left needles, lift the right stitch on the right needle over the left stitch and off the needle.

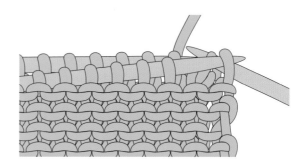

4. Repeat steps 2 and 3 to the end of the seam.

Three-Needle I-Cord Bind Off

Also called seam bind off

A variation of the three-needle bind off, this technique creates an I-cord along the seam that is thicker and more decorative than the ridge made with the three-needle bind off. You can vary the width of the I-cord by increasing or decreasing the number of I-cord stitches.

Three-needle I-cord bind off

1. With the right side of one of the pieces to be bound off facing you, cast on three stitches using the knitted cast on as follows: *Knit the first stitch but leave it on the left needle. Rotate the right needle clockwise, insert the tip of the left needle into the stitch from left to right, and remove the right needle; repeat from * two more times. These three stitches are the I-cord stitches.

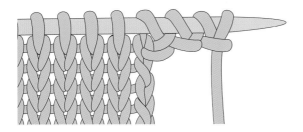

2. Place together the two pieces to be bound off, wrong sides together, with the needle with the I-cord stitches in front. The needles will be parallel with their tips pointing toward the right.

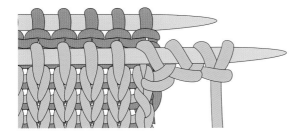

3. With a third needle, knit two I-cord stitches and slip the third to the right needle as if to purl.

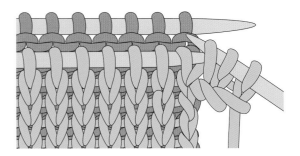

4. Insert the right needle into the first stitch on each needle and knit the two stitches together.

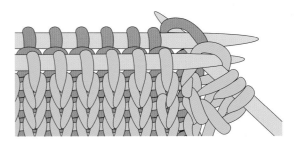

5. With one of the left needles, lift the second stitch in from the needle tip over the stitch closest to the tip and off the needle. Place the front left needle and the right needle tips together and slip the three I-cord stitches back to the front left needle.

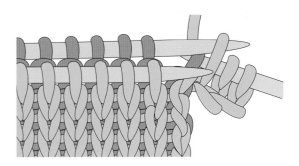

6. Repeat steps 3–5 until only the I-cord stitches remain. Lift the middle stitch over the left stitch and off the needle. Then lift the right stitch over the left and off the needle.

Knitting Off

Knitting off is a handy way to join a piece still on the needle to a knitted selvage, for example to join a sleeve to the body. It makes a tidy seam that's not very bulky.

A special selvage is not required. To ensure a neat seam, be sure to insert the needle between the edge and second stitch on the piece not on the needle. If you used a chain-stitch selvage (see page 10), you'll join two rows on the selvage with one stitch on the needle, so you may need to make adjustments.

Knitted-off seam joins two pieces knitted in different directions.

1. End one piece with a wrong-side row and keep the stitches on the needle. Break the yarn, leaving a long tail for sewing. Bind off the other piece.

2. Place the two pieces with right sides together, with the stitches on the needle in back.

3. Insert the right needle under the edge stitch on the front piece and into the first stitch on the needle. Knit the stitch with the tail and pull the loop through to the front.

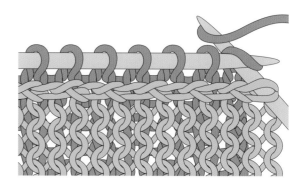

4. Insert the needle under the next edge stitch and into the next stitch on the needle, knit the stitch, and pull the loop through.

5. Lift the right stitch over the left and off the needle.

6. Repeat steps 4 and 5 to end of piece.

Sewn Seams

While there are times when a knitted or crocheted seam is the perfect choice, knitters most often sew their seams with yarn and a tapestry or yarn needle. You have a lot of options when it comes to sewn seams, but below are some guidelines that apply to all variations of sewn seams. Break away from using the same method all the time. Learn others so that you have choices to create the perfect seam for every project.

BEFORE YOU BEGIN

Choosing the optimal yarn, needle, sewing-strand length, and stitch type all contribute to how easy, or challenging, it is to sew seams.

Yarn Choice

In general, the project yarn is the best choice for sewing seams. Its thickness, elasticity, and drape will match that of the garment. It will also have the same blocking and cleaning requirements. However, there are times when the project yarn isn't the best choice:

- **Thick, bulky yarn** will produce thick, bulky seams. If it's plied, try separating the plies and use just one or two of them for sewing.
- **Loosely spun yarns** are also not a good choice for seams. They are likely to untwist during sewing, pull apart and break, producing a weak seam.
- **Novelty yarns,** too, are generally not suitable for sewing, as their texture can make it difficult to pull the yarn through.

When your project yarn is not appropriate for sewing, choose a plain yarn of the same color. If you can't find the exact color, go a shade darker rather than lighter. Darker colors are less likely to stand out. Needlepoint wool is a good choice because it's sturdy and comes in a wide range of colors, so you should be able to find the right one.

Sewing Needles

It's best to use a yarn needle, also called a darning needle, for sewing seams. Their blunt ends and large eyes are designed specifically for this purpose. The blunt end will go under or around stitches, not through them. Tapestry needles are not appropriate, as they're sharp and, unless used carefully, will split stitches. When weaving in ends, though, a pointy tapestry needle can be an asset. See "Weaving in Ends" on page 18.

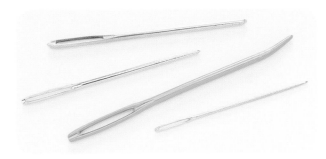

Yarn needles come in different sizes, lengths, and with different eye openings.

Length of Sewing Strand

Several shorter sewing strands are usually better than one long one. Keeping your sewing strand to 18" or less prevents the yarn from wearing and fraying as it's repeatedly pulled through the fabric. Fraying results in weak seams.

As you sew, try to keep an even tension, matching that of the knitted fabric. If your tension is too tight, the seam will be tight, less elastic, and restrict movement. It can also cause the seam to pucker and be unsightly.

Having a gap or unevenness at the start of a seam, such as at the bottom of a sweater, gives the finished piece a less-than-professional look. Here are two ways to avoid that gap. With either one, if you're not using a cast-on tail for your seam, leave about a 5" tail on your sewing strand and weave in the end later.

Figure Eight Start

1. Place pieces flat with the right sides face up and the edges to be joined next to each other. Insert the threaded needle into the corner stitch just above the cast-on edge of the piece without the tail from back to front.
2. Insert the needle into the corner stitch on the other piece from back to front to make a figure eight through both corner stitches.

Figure eight start

3. Pull the yarn snug to bring the edges together.

Loop Start

The same loop closure also can be used to tie off the sewing strand at the end of the seam.

1. Make a loop by inserting the threaded needle up through the corner stitch on the side without the tail, then back down through the same stitch, creating a loop about ½" long.

2. Insert the needle up through the corner stitch on the other side, then through the loop.

3. Pull the yarn to close the loop, and then pull the rest of the yarn through.

Stitch Choice

When considering stitches for a seam, you have many choices, and there will be at least one that is appropriate for your particular situation. The first consideration is whether you plan to sew from the right or the wrong side of your work.

Then you need to consider what you want the seam to look like. Do you want the seam to disappear so that your garment appears seamless? Or do you want the seam to be a visible and decorative design element? Is it important that the seam lies flat? There's at least one stitch ideally suited for every need.

SEAMS WORKED FROM THE RIGHT SIDE

The following seams are worked from the right side. Seams worked from the wrong side begin on page 48.

Decorative Raised Seam

Also called soft-seam stitch

Worked on bound-off edges, a decorative raised seam makes a strong, even seam that's the least bulky of the sewn seams. It's particularly good for shoulder seams and sock toes. It produces a raised edge on the right side that becomes a design element, especially when you use a contrasting-color yarn. On the wrong side, the seam is very flat.

1. Place the pieces flat with the right sides face up and the edges to be joined next to each other.

2. Insert the threaded needle under the outer half of the edge stitch on both pieces and pull the yarn through.

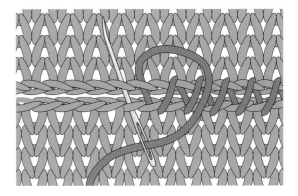

3. Move one stitch to the left and repeat step 2.
4. Repeat step 3 to the end of the seam.

When using contrasting yarn worked under the inner half of the edge stitches, a totally different look results.

Decorative raised seam worked under inner half of stitches

Decorative raised seam worked with contrasting yarn under inner half of stitches

Fishbone Stitch

Also called baseball stitch

Worked between two bound-off edges, the fishbone stitch creates a seam that is slightly raised and appears braided.

Fishbone-stitch seam

1. Lay the pieces flat with the right sides up and the edges to be joined together.
2. Insert the threaded needle under the right side of the edge stitch on the right piece from left to right and pull the yarn through. Then insert the needle under both sides of the edge stitch on the left piece from left to right and pull the yarn through.

3. Move up one stitch and repeat step 2; continue in this manner to the end of the seam.

You can also work under both sides of both edge stitches.

Mattress Stitch

Also called ladder stitch, invisible seam, weaving, woven seam, vertical grafting, running-thread seam, running-stitch seam

The mattress stitch is probably the most commonly used stitch for joining seams when there are an equal number of stitches or rows on the two pieces being joined. It creates a flexible yet strong seam that is virtually invisible on the right side with a slight ridge on the wrong side. The stitch is especially good when you want a straight edge along a column of knit stitches, for example on a raglan sleeve. Since it's worked on the right side, you can easily see what is happening as you sew, so it makes matching up colorwork and pattern stitches while seaming easy to do. Just remember to add selvage stitches to your pieces as you knit them.

The mattress stitch is also the most versatile stitch. It can be used with any pattern stitch, including ribbings. It can also be used to join all types of edges. For some seams, however, for example when joining selvages to bound-off edges, you'll need to fudge a little bit because knit stitches are wider than they are tall.

All versions of the mattress stitch can be worked under one or two bars, depending on how tight you want your seam. Working under every bar will give a tight, solid seam while working under two bars will give you a slightly looser seam.

Similarly, you can work a half stitch or a whole stitch in from the edge. Working in a whole stitch will make a stronger seam.

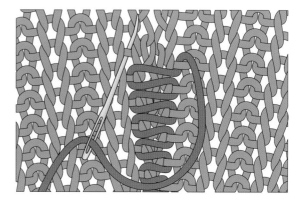

Mattress stitch worked a whole stitch in from the edge

If your knit edge is quite even and doesn't curl much, you might want to work just half a stitch in to give you a slightly less bulky seam. If your yarn is thick, you should definitely work just half a stitch in.

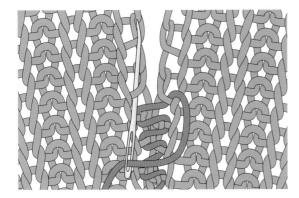

Mattress stitch worked a half stitch in from the edge

One of the beauties of the mattress stitch is that on any kind of seam, you can take up slack easily by picking up one bar on one side and two bars on the other once or twice to even the sides.

To ensure the tension of the seam matches your knitted tension, it's best to work the mattress stitch loosely for 1" or so and then gently, but firmly, pull the yarn snug but not too tight to close up the seam. Then work another inch and repeat.

Selvage to Selvage

Work both pieces being joined with stockinette-stitch selvage stitches.

Selvage-to-selvage seam

1. Lay the pieces flat with the right sides up and the edges to be joined together.
2. Insert the threaded needle under the horizontal bar between the first and second stitch on one piece, then insert the needle under the corresponding bar and the bar above it on the other piece.

3. Insert the needle under the next two horizontal bars on the first piece, then under the next two bars on the other, making sure each time to insert the needle into the same space where the yarn comes out from the previous stitch.
4. Repeat step 3 to the end of the seam. After working a few stitches, pull the yarn gently to bring the edges together, but not so tight as to create a pucker.

Selvage to Bound-Off Edge

Also called invisible vertical-to-horizontal seam

This method works well for attaching sleeves to the body of a sweater, especially a sweater with drop shoulders, or for sewing a front to a shoulder saddle. It's a little more difficult to work, because the ratio of stitches (on the bound-off edge) to rows (on the selvage) is not 1 to 1. Since there are always more rows to the inch than stitches, you will always end up with a fraction, because the number of stitches per inch (the smaller number) is divided by the number of rows per inch (the larger number).

A good rule of thumb is to pick up one stitch on the bound-off edge for every two rows on the selvage. The frequency of stitches to rows will depend on your yarn and the tension of your knitting. You may need to alternate between sewing one stitch to one row and sewing one stitch to two rows to yield a smoother seam. There may even be cases where you'll need to sew two stitches for every three rows, although the seam might be a bit loose.

Selvage seamed to bound-off edge

1. Place the pieces flat with the right sides up and the edges to be joined together.

2. For a 1:2 ratio (one stitch to two rows), insert the threaded needle under the edge stitch on the bound-off edge, then under two horizontal bars on the selvage, and pull the yarn through.

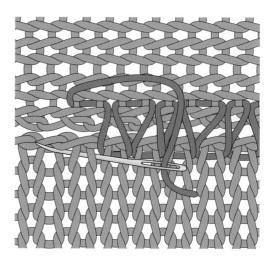

3. Repeat step 2 to the end of the seam.

If you want to forget the math and wing it, work one stitch to one row (bar). Every third or fourth stitch, insert the needle under two horizontal bars on the selvage to compensate for the uneven dimensions of knit stitches. The frequency may depend on your yarn and the tension of your knitting, so experiment to see what looks best.

Selvage to Live Stitches

Instead of binding off, you can work with live stitches to make a less bulky seam. I find it best to work with the live stitches on the needle, but you can also transfer the stitches to waste yarn.

Selvage seamed to live stitches

1. Set up as for working with a selvage to bound-off edge (see page 44).
2. Insert the threaded needle into the first live stitch from back to front, then under the horizontal bar of the corresponding stitch on the other piece. Insert the needle into the first live stitch again from front to back.

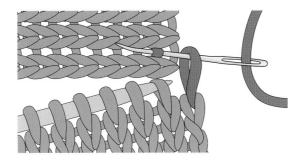

3. Repeat step 2 to the end of the seam. Depending on your yarn, you may have to insert the needle under two horizontal bars on the selvage, or alternate between one and two bars to keep the stitches straight.

Bound-Off Edge to Bound-Off Edge

Also called end-to-end seam, invisible horizontal seam

Mattress stitch is a good method for joining shoulder seams, but don't pull the yarn too tight or the seam will be quite rigid. Try to keep the same tension you used in knitting the piece so that the seam looks like a row of stockinette stitches.

For some yarns, this stitch is not a good choice. Dense yarns create stiff edges that don't pull under nicely, resulting in a depression along the seam that doesn't steam out.

Bound-off edge seamed to bound-off edge

1. Lay the pieces flat with the right sides up and the edges to be joined one above the other.
2. Insert the threaded needle under both sides of the stitch above the bound-off edge on one piece, then into the center of the corresponding stitch below the bound-off edge on the other piece and up into the center of the stitch to its left.

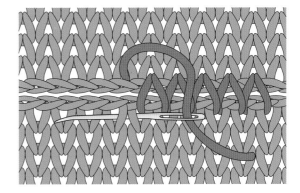

3. Repeat step 2 to the end of the seam, working from right to left, always inserting the needle into the same hole that the yarn came out of on the previous stitch.

Bound-Off Edge to Live Stitches

You can also use mattress stitch to join bound-off stitches to live stitches along the shoulder. Bind off the back stitches, but leave the front stitches on the needle. Use the bound-off tail or a new strand rather than the end of the yarn on the knitting needle for sewing.

Bound-off edge seamed to live stitches

1. Lay the pieces flat with right sides up and the edges to be joined one above the other.
2. Insert the threaded needle into the first live stitch from back to front, then under both sides of the first bound-off stitch.

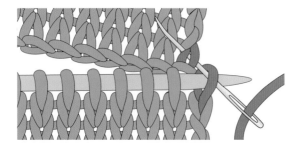

3. Insert the needle back into the same live stitch from front to back and slip the stitch off the needle.

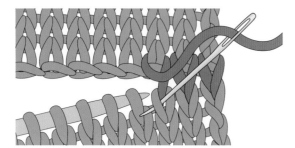

4. Repeat steps 2 and 3 to the end of the seam.

Reverse Stockinette Stitch

When seaming reverse stockinette stitch, it's best to work under a stitch on every row instead of every two. Even so, it can be difficult to get a seam that blends in perfectly.

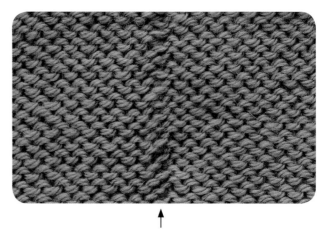

Seamed reverse-stockinette stitch

1. Lay the pieces flat with the right sides up and the edges to be joined together.
2. Insert the threaded needle under the lower bump between the last two stitches on one side, then under the upper bump of the edge stitch on the other side.

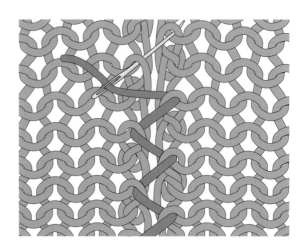

3. Repeat step 2 to the end of the seam.

Garter Stitch

Also called garter-stitch seam

Worked closer to the seam than on reverse stockinette stitch, mattress stitch on garter stitch meshes two pieces together to make a flat seam. Do not use a selvage stitch if you plan on using this technique.

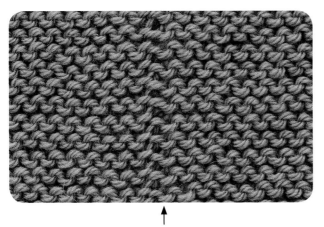

Garter-stitch seam

1. Lay the pieces flat with the right sides up and the edges to be joined together side by side.
2. Insert the threaded needle under the lower purl bump between the last two stitches on one piece, then under the upper bump of the edge stitch on the corresponding ridge on the other piece.

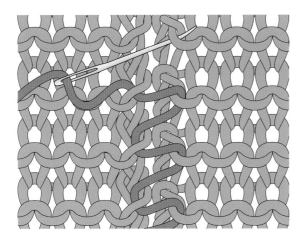

3. Repeat step 2.

⟶ Pattern Stitch ⟶

To join pieces with a pattern stitch, knit both pieces using an added chain-stitch selvage (see page 10), and use the selvage-to-selvage seam to join the pieces (see page 43).

Seams are less noticeable in ribbed areas if they're made just after a raised knit stitch. If you work the rib on an even number of stitches, each piece will begin with a knit stitch and end with a purl, setting you up nicely to work the mattress stitch between the first and second stitches on each edge.

If your pattern calls for an odd number of stitches, or your cast on gives you an odd number of stitches so that the edge stitch on both pieces is a knit stitch, you can work the seam using half the edge stitch on both sides. See "Mattress Stitch" on page 42. Or you can work the ribbing on one less stitch than called for in the pattern and increase one when the ribbing is finished.

Seams Worked from the Wrong Side

Not as widely used as seams worked from the right side, these methods do have their place.

Edge-to-Edge Seam

Worked from side to side along the edges, this method results in a seam that lies flat, but it's not particularly strong. It's best when used with stockinette stitch, creating a relatively inconspicuous seam that is quite stretchy. The pieces being joined should have the same number of rows. Don't use selvage stitches.

Edge-to-edge seam

1. Place pieces face down with the edges to be joined next to each other.
2. Working from side to side, insert the threaded needle through the little knots of the edge stitches on each side.

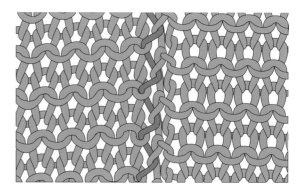

Backstitch

When you don't need to match pieces row for row, the backstitch is a good technique when you want the seam to be durable or provide stability, for example on a bag or jacket. It produces a strong seam that is easy and quick to work, but it's not as elastic as others. The seam can also be bulky, so it's best for use with lightweight yarns. For a less bulky seam, work the backstitch with live stitches (see page 50). Because you can't see what's happening on the right side of your fabric, this technique isn't a good choice for pattern stitches, colorwork, or when it's important to match both pieces row for row.

Backstitch is usually worked just inside the edge, especially with thick fabrics. For thinner fabric, you can work in from the edge through the first row of stitches. By working in from the edge you can take up unwanted fullness, but keep the seam allowance to no more than 1" to prevent the seam from being too bulky.

The backstitch can be used to join selvage, cast-on, and bound-off edges. It does not require special selvages, but works well with the chain stitch (see page 10) and garter stitch (see page 11) selvages. Use chain-stitch selvages if stitching under the edge stitches. The garter stitch and beaded selvages are best when sewing below the edge, as the selvage stitches are clearly demarcated and you can easily insert the needle between the selvage stitch and the next stitch to make a nice, straight seam. You need to carefully place your needle to create neat, even seams.

Backstitch seam

1. Pin the pieces with right sides together.

2. Insert the threaded needle under the edge stitch on both pieces from front to back. Move to the left about ½", insert the needle under the edge stitches on both pieces from back to front, and pull the yarn through.

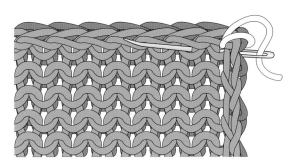

3. Move to the right of where the yarn comes out on the previous stitch and repeat step 2.

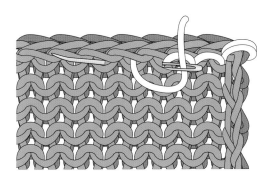

4. Repeat steps 2 and 3 to the end of the seam.

Backstitch Using Live Stitches

The backstitch can also be worked with live stitches. It's helpful to keep the stitches on the needles, dropping them off as you work them.

Backstitch seam using live stitches

1. Place the pieces with right sides together with the needles pointing to the right.

2. Insert the threaded needle into the first stitch on both pieces from front to back.

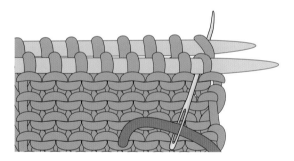

3. Insert the needle into the next stitch on both pieces to the left from back to front and pull the yarn through.

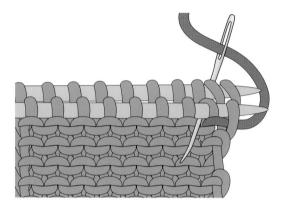

4. Insert the needle again into the stitches to the right from front to back, passing the needle above the yarn from the previous stitch. Pull the yarn through and drop the stitches from the needle. Then move two stitches to the left and insert the needle into these stitches from back to front and pull the yarn through.

5. Repeat step 4 to the end of the seam.

Flat Seam

As its name suggests, this stitch creates a flat seam that makes it a good choice for joining two selvages, such as button bands and borders.

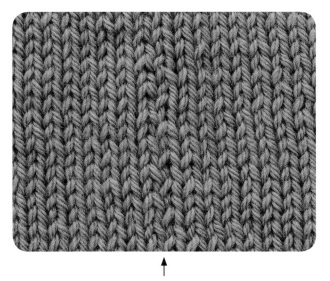

Flat seam

1. With right sides together, insert the threaded needle under the edge stitches on both pieces from front to back, and pull the yarn through.

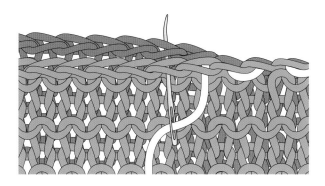

2. Move to the left, insert the needle under the edge stitches on both pieces from back to front, and pull the yarn through.

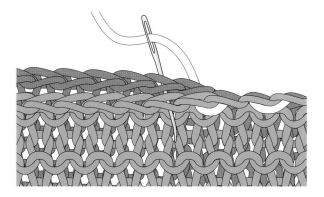

3. Move to the left, insert the needle under the edges stitches on both pieces from front to back, and pull the yarn through.

4. Repeat steps 2 and 3 to the end of the seam.

Free-Loop Slip Stitch

This stitch is useful for sewing hems on pieces worked from the top down. The live stitches will still be on the knitting needle.

Free-loop slip stitch

1. Fold the hem to the wrong side and hold the knitting needle against the main fabric.

2. Insert the threaded needle under one strand of the main fabric from top to bottom, then from back to front through the first live stitch on the needle, and slip the stitch from the needle.

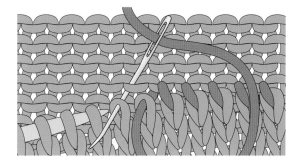

3. Repeat step 2 to the end of the seam.

Stitch-by-Stitch Seam

A variation of the free-loop slip stitch (page 51), the stitch-by-stitch seam makes a neat hem. A slight ridge is created on the right side, especially if you work too tightly. You'll need to work with live stitches, so use a provisional cast on when beginning the piece.

Stitch-by-stitch seam, right side

Stitch-by-stitch seam, wrong side

1. Fold the hem to the wrong side and pin in place.
2. Insert the threaded needle into the first live stitch from back to front and pull the yarn through.
3. Insert the needle from bottom to top under the lower purl bump immediately above the live stitch, then down through the next lower purl bump, and pull the yarn through.

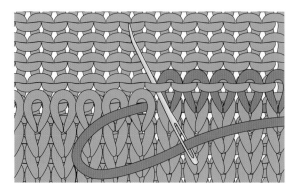

4. Insert the needle into the same live stitch from front to back, then into the next live stitch from back to front, and pull the yarn through.

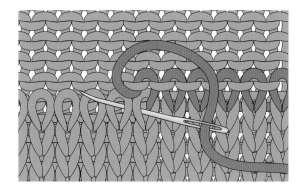

5. Repeat steps 3 and 4 to the end of the seam. Be sure to insert the needle up under the same purl bump the yarn came under on the previous stitch and follow the line of purl bumps across the hem.

SEAMS WORKED FROM EITHER SIDE

Depending on the desired look, the following stitches can be worked on either the right or wrong side.

Whipstitch

Also called overcasting, overcast seam, overstitch, over sewing, flat seam

The whipstitch creates a stretchier seam than many sewn stitches and is often recommended for use in fine lace knitting. When worked on the wrong side, it creates a flat seam, which is particularly good for joining borders since the stitches don't show on the front. It's also good for joining button bands and collars that have been knit separately, and for hems.

The whipstitch can be worked in two ways, one for lace knitting and one for denser knitting. For lace, insert the threaded needle under the inner half of the edge stitches. This makes an open, flat seam suitable for lace, but an ugly seam for denser knitting. For all knitting other than lace, insert the needle under the outer half of the edge stitches. Worked this way, the seam is slightly thicker.

Whipstitch seam worked on wrong side

1. Place the two pieces with their right sides together.
2. Insert the needle under the inner half of the edge stitch on one side from back to front and then under the inner half of the edge stitch on the other piece from back to front. For lace knitting, insert the needle under the inner half of the edge stitches.

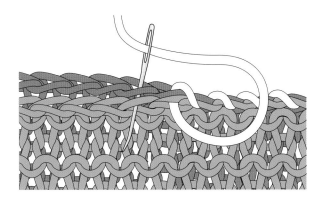

3. Repeat step 2 to the end of the seam.

When worked on the right side, the whipstitch produces a decorative, cordlike seam, especially when sewn with contrasting yarn. It's best to use a sewing yarn thicker than the project yarn to cover the edges of the seam. It can be used with or without selvage stitches but creates a tighter seam without them.

*Whipstitch worked on right side
with contrasting yarn*

1. Place the pieces side by side with right sides up and the edges to be joined next to each other.
2. Insert the needle under the inner half of the edge stitch on one piece from front to back, then under the inner half of the edge stitch on the other piece from back to front. Pull the yarn through, but not too tightly or the seam will not lie flat.

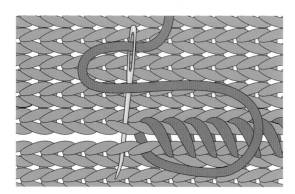

3. Repeat step 2 with the next pair of edge stitches to the end of the seam.

Slip Stitch

Also called hemstitch

Because the slip stitch doesn't make as strong a seam as other stitches, it's not suitable for seams that will take a great deal of stress or wear. It's good for joining two pieces when one goes on top of the other, for example, for hems, patch pockets, or pocket linings. Work as close to the edge as possible and sew loosely so the seam won't be too tight.

The slip stitch can be worked with chain-stitch selvage (see page 10) on the top piece, but you'll have to catch every other stitch on the bottom piece, which might make for a slightly more open seam.

Slip-stitch seam

1. Place one piece on top of the other and pin them together. If working a hem, fold the hem to the wrong side and pin it in place.
2. Catch the side of a stitch or the horizontal bar between two stitches on the bottom piece, then the side of a stitch from the top piece.

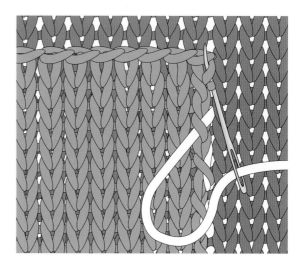

3. Repeat step 2 to the end of the seam, being sure to work along the same column of stitches on the bottom piece to keep the seam straight.

Kitchener Stitch

The Kitchener stitch is a way to join two pieces of knitting seamlessly. The join is invisible, but it doesn't provide the strength or stability of a seam. It's commonly used to join toe stitches when knitting socks from the cuff down, but you can use it whenever you want to join two pieces seamlessly with live stitches. It's most effective with stockinette stitch and garter stitches, but you can use it with pattern stitches as well. It can be worked with the stitches on or off the needles. *Also called grafting.*

For Stockinette Stitch on Needles

When moving between needles, bring the yarn under the needle tips on the right.

When I do the Kitchener stitch, I chant the following to myself for steps 2–5: knit, purl, purl, knit. I've also heard knitters say: knit, slip, purl, purl, slip, knit. Either works quite well to keep you on track.

Kitchener stitch for stockinette stitch; white stitches are the sewn ones.

1. End one piece with a right-side row. Break the yarn, leaving a long tail, and thread it onto a yarn needle. Hold the two needles parallel to each other with the wrong sides together and the working strand on the right of the back needle. Insert the threaded needle into the first stitch on the front needle as if to purl, and then into the first stitch on the back needle as if to knit.

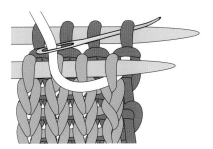

2. Insert the needle into the first stitch on the front needle as if to knit, pull the yarn through, and drop the stitch from the knitting needle.

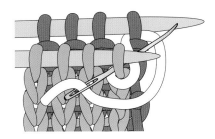

3. Insert the needle into the next stitch on the front needle as if to purl, and pull the yarn through, leaving the stitch on the needle.

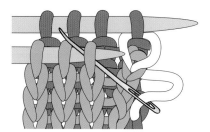

4. Insert the needle into the first stitch on the back needle as if to purl, pull the yarn through, and drop the stitch from the knitting needle.

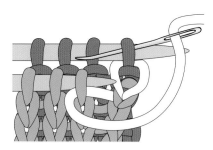

5. Insert the needle into the next stitch on the back needle as if to knit, and pull the yarn through, leaving the stitch on the needle.

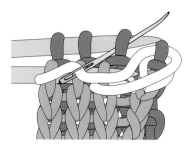

6. Repeat steps 2–5 to the end of the seam.

For Stockinette Stitch off Needles

Generally, remove the stitches from the needles all at once, especially if there aren't very many. If you have lots of stitches, or are afraid you may lose a stitch, you can slip them off the needles as you work.

1. Break the yarn, leaving a long tail, and thread it onto a yarn needle. Place the two pieces to be joined on a flat surface with right sides facing up and the needles next to and parallel to each other, with the pieces extending away from each other. The yarn tail is on the right end of the upper piece. Carefully remove the knitting needles. Insert the threaded yarn needle into the first stitch on the lower piece from back to front and pull the yarn through; then insert the needle into the first stitch on the upper piece from back to front and pull the yarn through.

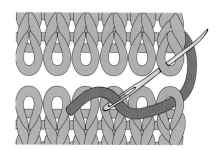

2. Insert the needle into the already worked stitch on the lower piece from front to back, then into the next stitch from back to front, and pull the yarn through.

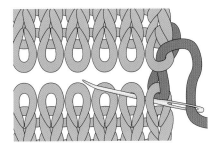

3. Insert the needle into the stitch already worked on the upper piece from front to back, then into the next stitch from back to front, and pull the yarn through.

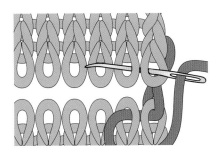

4. Repeat steps 2 and 3 to the end of the seam.

For Garter Stitch on Needles

Set up as in step 1 of Kitchener stitch for stockinette stitch on needles. See page 55.

Kitchener stitch for garter stitch; white stitches are the sewn ones.

1. With the knit row of the front needle facing the purl row of the back needle and the working strand on the right of the back needle, insert the needle into the first stitch on the front needle as if to purl, and pull the yarn through. Then insert the needle into the first stitch on the back needle as if to purl, and pull the yarn through.

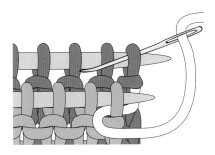

2. Insert the needle into the first stitch on the front needle as if to knit. Pull the yarn through and slip the stitch off the needle.

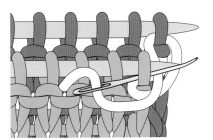

3. Insert the needle into the next stitch on the front needle as if to purl and pull the yarn through, leaving the stitch on the knitting needle.

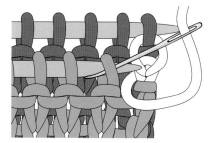

4. Insert the needle into the first stitch on the back needle as if to knit, pull the yarn through, and slip the stitch off the knitting needle.

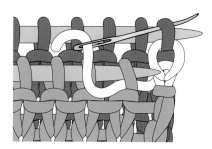

5. Insert the needle into the next stitch on the back needle as if to purl and pull the yarn through, leaving the stitch on the knitting needle.

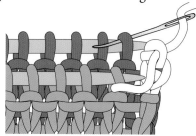

6. Repeat steps 2–5 to the end of the row.

For Garter Stitch off Needles

Set up as in step 1 of Kitchener stitch for stockinette stitch off needles (page 56) with the knit row of the top needle facing up and the purl row of the lower needle facing up.

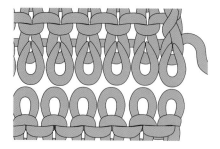

1. Insert the needle into the first stitch on the lower piece from back to front, and pull the yarn through.

2. Insert the needle into the first stitch on the upper piece from front to back, and pull the yarn through.

3. Insert the needle into the already worked stitch on the lower piece from front to back, then into the next stitch from back to front, and pull the yarn through.

4. Insert the needle into the already worked stitch on the upper piece from back to front, then into the next stitch from front to back, and pull the yarn through.

5. Repeat steps 4 and 5 to the end of the row.

For K1, P1 Ribbing

Sometimes you need to join two pieces of ribbing that have been worked in opposite directions. Although Kitchener stitch doesn't duplicate a row of ribbing exactly, it's useful for avoiding a bulky seam, for example, when joining front bands at the back of the neck. You'll need four double-pointed needles for this technique.

Kitchener stitch for knit one, purl one ribbing; white stitches are the sewn ones.

1. On each piece, place all the knit stitches on one needle and all the purl stitches on another.

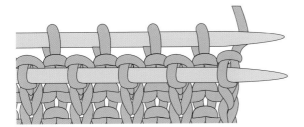

2. With right sides together, graft together the knit stitches on both pieces using the Kitchener stitch for stockinette stitch.

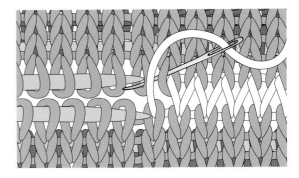

3. Turn the work over and with wrong sides together, graft the remaining stitches as in step 2.

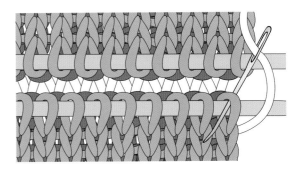

Picking Up Stitches

Sometimes it's necessary to add extra stitches or rows to a piece to finish it, for example, when adding a border, edging, or collar. Adding rows can also be part of the pattern stitch itself, as with entrelac knitting. Picking up stitches (sometimes called picking up and knitting stitches) along a knit edge enables you to create a new row of stitches.

Stitches are usually picked up on the right side of the work so that you can see exactly what you're doing. This enables you to make neat, straight joins. It's possible to pick up from the wrong side, although it's a little trickier to do so evenly.

Picking up stitches (abbreviated in instructions as PU) is usually done with a knitting needle, but a crochet hook can also be used. Many advocate using a needle at least one or two sizes smaller than your project needle to facilitate picking up the stitches, then switching back to the project needles to work the first row. This works well, but can create a row of smaller stitches along the picked-up row. Depending on your yarn, this can make the join slightly less flexible than the rest of your piece. I find using the project needles for picking up stitches works quite well. Use your swatch to experiment to see what works best for you. What works well with one yarn may not work as well with another.

The use and choice of selvage stitches can help you make a neat, crisp edge. See "Selvage Stitches" on page 9.

Some knitters like to anchor the picked-up tail by wrapping it around the needle along with the working yarn when picking up the second stitch. On the next row, knit the two loops together as one stitch.

Spacing Ratio

Picked-up stitches should be spaced as evenly as possible to prevent the puckering of either piece. There's no hard-and-fast rule about the ratio of picked-up stitches per row or stitches. It depends on many factors: your needles, yarn, gauge, pattern stitch, and the look that you want. Patterns often give you a number of stitches to pick up, but the number should be regarded as a guide. Your gauge and knitting may differ from that of the designer, especially if you're using a substitute yarn. A stitch or two isn't going to make a difference on the pick-up row; you can increase or decrease stitches in the first row to get to the number of stitches required in the pattern.

Knitting can be pulled out of shape by too many stitches picked up (left) and too few stitches picked up (right).

If your pattern specifies a number of stitches to pick up, you can space the stitches evenly by marking the middle of the edge with a removable marker. Then divide each half in half again with a marker. If a quarter of the length is still too long, divide it again into eighths. Then divide the number of stitches to be picked up by the number of sections between the markers to give you the number of stitches to be picked up in each section.

If the patterns doesn't specify a number, a rule of thumb is to pick up three stitches for every four rows along a stockinette-stitch selvage. Because garter stitch is more compact, pick up one stitch for every two rows along a garter-stitch selvage. The important thing is to maintain your gauge when picking up stitches to achieve a smooth join that doesn't pucker.

One sure way to ensure you keep to gauge is to place a pin or marker every inch along the edge where you'll be picking up stitches. Pick up the number of stitches in your gauge between each pair of pins. For example, if your gauge is 20 stitches over 4", you should pick up five stitches between each pair of pins. You can always use your swatch to determine which ratio works best for your yarn. See "Planning" on page 8.

Picking Up Stitches along Straight Edges

To pick up stitches along a straight edge, some people like to use a knitting needle while others find it easier to do with a crochet hook. Instructions for both methods are given here.

Needle Method

When picking up stitches along a selvage, insert the needle between the first (or selvage) and second stitches. Make sure that you always insert the needle between these two columns of stitches to ensure a straight join. If you used a chain-stitch selvage, insert the needle under both sides of the selvage stitch.

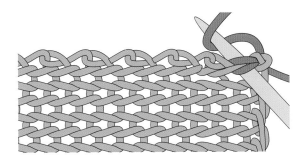

If your edge stitches are loose and you find picking up stitches creates holes along the edge, you can use a slightly different method. Pick up the far side of the edge stitch with the left needle and pick up a stitch with the right needle by knitting through the back of the loop on the left needle. The twisted edge stitches make a tighter join.

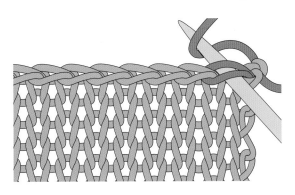

When picking up stitches along a bound-off edge, insert the needle under both sides of the edge stitch.

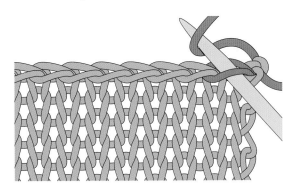

For thick, chunky yarns, you may find it easier to go under only the inner side of the edge stitch. You can also pick up through the stitches in the row below the edge, but this will result in a thicker ridge on the back of your work.

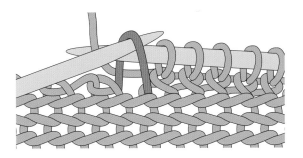

With garter stitch, pick up stitches between the ridges where there's a convenient hole to the left of the ridge strand extending down from the edge.

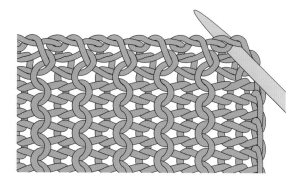

Hook Method

If you prefer to use a crochet hook, insert the hook under the edge stitch, pull the loop through, and place it on the needle.

Picking up stitches with a crochet hook

Picking up stitches is generally done from the right side, working from right to left, so the first row of knitting will be a wrong-side row.

If you want the first row of knitting to be a right-side row, pick up the stitches working from left to right. With the wrong side facing you, insert the needle from back to front under the edge stitch, wrap the yarn around the needle, and pull it through to the back on the right side.

Picking up stitches from left to right with a needle from the wrong side

If this is awkward for you, work on the right side and use a crochet hook to pull the yarn through; then transfer the loops to a knitting needle.

Picking up stitches from left to right with a hook from the right side

Picking Up Stitches along Shaped Edges

It's a little more challenging to pick up stitches along shaped edges. If your shaping has created a stepped edge, alternate between picking up stitches under the edge stitches and through stitches a row or two in from the edge. This takes a little care to make sure that the picked-up edge is straight or nicely curved.

Picking up stitches along a stepped edge; some are at the edge while others are in from the edge.

The technique name "pick up and knit" is a misnomer. Directions will say pick up and knit a certain number of stitches, but they don't mean pick up a stitch and then knit it. You are just pulling a loop through onto the needle to create a new stitch as though you were knitting.

⟶ Picking Up Twice ⟵

Sometimes you need to pick up more than one stitch per stitch or row. To do this, pick up one stitch by inserting the needle under the far side of an edge stitch; then pick up another under both sides of the same stitch before moving on.

Picking Up Stitches in the Middle of Work

Stitches can be picked up in the middle of a piece, which is useful if you want to add a piece, such as a patch pocket, seamlessly to another. You can use either a needle or hook to do this. Insert the needle or hook into the center of a stitch in the fabric, pull a loop through the stitch from the back, and place it on a needle. Be sure to insert the needle or hook between the same column or row of stitches each time to keep the edge straight. You might find basting a line of contrasting-colored thread helps you keep the edge straight.

Picking up stitches in the middle of a piece

Bands

Bands are important elements in knitted pieces, serving several functions. Most important, they strengthen and support the edges. Bands keep edges from curling and sagging, helping to maintain the shape of the entire piece. In garments, bands also provide a place for buttons and other closures, such as snaps, hooks, clips, and frogs. Bands worked in a different pattern stitch or contrasting color can nicely set off the pattern stitches and colors of the main portion of the piece.

The most commonly used stitches for bands are ribbing, garter stitch, and seed stitch, mainly because they're non-curling, but also because they're decorative. There's no reason why you can't use other stitches, especially for decorative bands. Lace borders nicely dress up the bottom edges or cuffs of a sweater. They're also commonly added to lace shawls to finish the edges. The stitch choice is a design decision and will depend largely on your piece and the function of the band.

As the band can be a focal point, you want its edges to be as neat as possible. Adding a selvage stitch to the band will give you a neat finished edge. For example, work a simple chain-stitch selvage (see page 10) by slipping the edge stitch on every right-side row. If you're working your band in ribbing, add an extra stitch so you have an odd number of stitches. Then slip the first stitch on every right-side row.

Bands, especially button bands, are often knit as part of a garment and don't require any finishing. Many knitters use needles two sizes smaller than the project needles to knit bands, making them firmer and more structural. This can be difficult to do when knitting a vertical band as you knit your garment. If you like the look of a tighter band, or it works better with your yarn, knit the band separately and sew it on later.

If your band will be a button band, don't forget to make the buttonholes! See "Buttonholes" on page 85.

Semi-Attached Band

Semi-attached bands, usually for button bands on garments, require planning at the beginning of your project. You need to cast on the band stitches along with the stitches of the main piece and work the bottom band, including the vertical band stitches. Once the bottom band is knit, place the front band stitches on a holder and finish the rest of the piece. Adding a selvage stitch to the main piece after finishing the bottom band will facilitate sewing on the band later. See "Selvage Stitches" on page 9.

Seed-stitch band worked with a chain-stitch selvage

Place front band stitches on a holder to be worked later.

To work the band, place the stitches back onto needles. Attach the yarn, leaving a long tail for sewing, and cast on one stitch at the inside edge of the band. Work this stitch in stockinette stitch to provide a seam allowance. Knit the band until it's approximately the right length and leave the stitches on the needle in case you need to adjust the length of the band.

Thread the tail onto a yarn needle and use the mattress stitch (see page 42) to sew the band to the edge, matching row for row. If the band is the right length, the two top edges will match perfectly. If they don't, shorten or add to the band, then bind off.

Sew semi-attached band to the main piece.

Separate Band

Knit the main piece with a selvage stitch if the band will be attached to the selvage. See "Selvage Stitches" on page 9. If the band will be attached to a cast-on or bound-off edge, you won't need selvage stitches. Cast on the required number of stitches for the band plus one stitch. The extra stitch provides a seam allowance and should be worked in stockinette stitch on the edge of the band that will be joined to the main piece. Knit the band. Then pin it to the edge and sew it with the mattress stitch (see page 42) or one of the stitches that creates a flat seam (see page 51).

Sew a band knit separately to the main piece with the mattress stitch.

> ### ⟶ Bands ⟵
>
> Bands can add flair and distinction to your knitting. Their main function is to strengthen edges and prevent them from stretching or curling. At the same time, they can be a decorative design element. They can be added to any knitted edge and are generally smaller and thinner than bands.
>
> Bands can be worked in the project yarn to form a subtle edge or in contrasting yarn to make a bolder statement.

Picked-Up Bands

Rather than knitting a band and sewing it to the garment, you can pick up stitches along the garment edge to knit the band. You can pick up stitches along a selvage, cast-on, or bound-off edge.

Starting at the right corner, pick up and knit stitches along the edge, being careful to always pick up between the same two columns or rows of stitches. See "Picking Up Stitches" on page 60. Then knit the band and bind off.

Pick up stitches along the edge for a knitted-on band.

The tricky part to these bands is picking up the right number of stitches along the edge. Too many stitches make the band pucker. Too few, and the main piece will pucker. A rule of thumb is to pick up three stitches for every four rows of knitting. Experiment with your project yarn to see what works.

Garter stitch is a popular choice for horizontal bands as its ridges give a clean, crisp look. When using garter stitch, bind off the band on the wrong side. The bound-off edge will curl slightly to the back, creating a neat edge on the right side.

RS
bind off

WS
bind off

Garter-stitch band with edge bound off on right side (top) and on wrong side (bottom)

Applied Bands

Another option is to work an applied border while binding off. You can accomplish this with the edging bind off (below). For this, you need live stitches.

Band applied with edging bind off

Finish knitting your piece, ending with a wrong-side row, but don't bind off.

1. With the right side facing you, cast on the number of stitches needed for the band using the knit cast on as follows: *Knit the first stitch, but leave it on the left needle. Rotate the right needle clockwise, insert the tip of the left needle into the stitch from left to right, and remove the right needle. Repeat from * until you have cast on the band stitches.

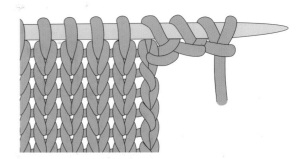

2. Work all but the last edging stitch in your band pattern. Depending on your pattern, knit two stitches together or purl two stitches together, working together the last edging stitch and the first stitch to be bound off. For some patterns, knitting through the back loops may make a neater join than knitting normally. Turn and

work the band stitches in pattern. Turn. Continue to repeat this step. The number of band stitches will always remain the same while the rest of the stitches will decrease.

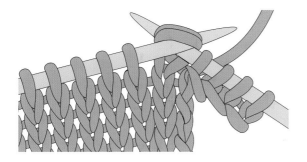

3. When only the band stitches remain, turn work and bind them off.

Neckbands

Neckbands are picked up and knit once the garment is finished. Because a neck edge involves both straight and shaped edges, picking up and knitting the right number of stitches takes a bit of thought, as different ratios of stitches will be required for the different edges. In general, pick up one stitch per stitch on a straight edge and two stitches for every three rows; on shaped edges, pick up three stitches for every four rows, depending on your yarn and gauge. See "Picking Up Stitches" on page 60. Then knit the band, either back and forth for a cardigan or in the round for a pullover.

Some patterns have you bind off the back neck stitches while others have you put live stitches on a holder. Bound-off stitches will give you a firmer edge; live stitches are more likely to stretch. Picking up stitches along the bound-off edge will also give your neckband better definition.

For a different look, you can knit the neckband twice as long as the finished band and fold it over to make a neat rolled edge, like a hem. Bind off the stitches and pin the bound-off edge to the inside of the neck edge, easing the curved edges together so they fit properly. This may require slightly stretching the bound-off edge to fit the neck. Then sew the edge of the band in place, matching the tension of the knitted fabric. If the seam is too tight, the opening could be difficult to get over your head. Because the seam around a neckline is generally a tight curve, use small, evenly spaced stitches. The whipstitch (see page 53) and slip stitch (see page 54) are good choices for sewing down the edge because they are less firm than other stitches. Sewing through the outer side of the bound-off stitches gives you a neat seam.

To avoid a tight edge, don't bind off when the band is finished. Leave the stitches on the needle, or you may find it easier to put them onto a piece of waste yarn. Fold over the neckband and pin the edge in place, easing the curved edges together. Use the free-loop slip stitch (see page 51) to sew the live stitches of the band in place, removing the waste yarn as you work.

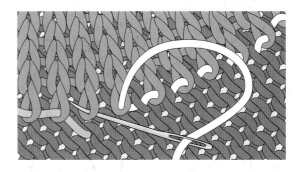

Folded neckband

The neckband can be knit as a separate piece that is then sewn on. I find this doesn't work very well, as the join between the neckband and the neck tends to be weak and allows the neckband to flop, but it would be good for attaching a collar. This technique may also work better with thicker yarns or yarns with more body.

Hems

Hems are essentially borders along the bottom of loosely hanging garments. They are folded back on themselves similar to some neckbands, creating a double layer. They can also be worked along the front edges of a garment, for example a cardigan or jacket, when you don't plan on using buttons. Hems aren't restricted to garments. They can also be worked as a finishing band on other projects, such as blankets, or be used as a casing for elastic or a drawstring.

Hems provide structure to a piece, but if too thick, they can add unwanted bulk and weight to the edge. To minimize the bulk, a hem is generally knit in stockinette stitch, and the portion turned under is worked on needles at least two sizes smaller than the project needles. However, this can make the hem firmer than the rest of your piece.

To avoid this firmness, decrease the number of stitches by 10% for the portion that folds under; then knit the hem on the project needles. Decrease stitches one row inside the fold line, that is, on the portion that will be turned under.

As with other seams, the one used to attach a hem should match the tension of the fabric—loose enough so that it gives with the fabric and doesn't show on the right side, but not so loose that the hem sags. If the stitches are too tight, an indented line will be visible on the right side, and the edge may bend along the seam line. To minimize the line, work with live stitches rather than a bound-off edge.

Be sure to fold the hem straight so that each stitch is sewed to stitches above it in the same column. If sewn to the column on either side of its own column, the hem will twist, and no amount of blocking or pressing will straighten it.

Fold Lines

The fold on a stockinette-stitch hem tends to be quite rounded. If you don't like this look, you can add a fold line to a hem so the folded edge lies as flat as possible. A fold line is worked at the turning point of the hem.

A stockinette hem without a fold line is rounded.

A tightly stitched hem leaves a deep indentation on the right side. Notice the row of purl stitches at the bottom, which creates a fold line.

Slip-Stitch Fold Line

A slipped stitch creates a fold line that's flatter than the stockinette-stitch hem, but not as sharp as the purl fold line. It's worked over an odd number of stitches.

Slip-stitch fold line as worked

Slip-stitch fold line folded

On a knit row, K1, *bring yarn to front and slip 1 purlwise, bring yarn to back and K1. Repeat from * across.

Purl Fold Line

A purl fold line makes a neat, flat edge. The purl bumps create a textured line along the bottom edge that can be accentuated, becoming a design element, if worked in a contrasting color.

At the turning point, purl a row on the right side or knit a row on the wrong side, then continue with stockinette stitch. The single purl ridge makes a neat line where the fabric naturally wants to fold.

Purl fold line as worked

Purl fold line folded

Picot Fold Line

Creating a decorative flat edge, the picot fold line is worked over an even number of stitches.

On a knit row, knit two stitches, *bring the yarn forward to the front to make a yarn over, and knit two stitches together. Repeat from * across to the last two stitches, yarn over, and knit two stitches. Then resume stockinette stitch for the rest of the hem.

Picot fold line as worked

Picot fold line folded

Working Hems

When adding a hem after the garment is finished, you have two choices. You can pick up stitches along the edge of the main piece, or you can extend the hem from live stitches along the edge. Either way, the hem is worked downward from the edge of the main piece.

Extended Hem

While easy to work, knitting an extended hem does require planning from the beginning of your project, as you'll need to use a provisional cast on for your main piece.

When ready to knit the hem, remove the provisional cast on and place the live stitches on the project needles. Work the outer half of the hem with the project needles; then work the fold line. Switch to needles that are two sizes smaller and knit the folded-over portion of the hem with the same number of rows as the first half.

You now have two options:

Bind off: Bind off all stitches, then fold the hem under and loosely pin it in place. Sew the edge of the hem to the wrong side of the main piece through the outer half of the edge stitches. The whipstitch (see page 53) and slip stitch (see page 54) are the best choices for sewing the hem.

Bound-off hem being sewn down

Don't bind off: With the stitches on the needle or a piece of waste yarn, fold the hem under and loosely pin it in place. Sew the hem to the wrong side of the main piece using the live stitches and the free-loop slip stitch (page 51) or the stitch-by-stitch seam (page 52), removing the needles or waste yarn as you go.

This method works particularly well for heavier and bulky yarns, as you won't have the added bulk of the bound-off edge.

Hem being sewn with live stitches

⟶ Steeked Edges ⟵

A steek is a method of bridging an opening, for example the front of a cardigan, when knitting in the round so that the body can be worked only with knit rows. During finishing, sew a row of machine stitching on each side of the steek cutting line. The tightness of the stitches won't show and will firmly secure the cut edges. Cut the knitted steek between the two rows of stitching, exposing the ragged edges that will be hidden when sandwiched between the two layers of the hem.

Picked-Up Hem

A picked-up hem is added to the bottom edge of the knitted piece, adding length to the garment equal to the depth of the hem. You can also use a picked-up hem to cover up cut or steeked edges. See "Steeked Edges" at left.

With the right side facing you and the project needles, pick up stitches along the edge of the main piece. Work the outer half of the hem and add a fold line. Switch to smaller needles and knit the folded-under portion so that when folded, the hem just meets the picked-up ridge on the wrong side. Sew the hem in place along the picked-up ridge using either of the techniques described previously for the extended hem on page 70.

Sew a picked-up hem in place along the pick-up ridge.

For steeks, be sure to pick up stitches outside the machine stitching (pink thread in photo) that secures the cut edge.

Pick up stitches along the edge of a steek.

Then knit the hem long enough to cover the stitching on the inside of the piece. This will firmly seal off the cut edge.

Fold the picked-up hem over and sew over the cut steek edge.

⮜ Securing Steeks with ⮞ Crochet Chain Stitches

If you prefer, you can secure the cut edges with a row of vertically chained stitches.

1. Insert a crochet hook into the center of a stitch, several stitches to one side of where the steek will be cut. Pull a loop through.

2. Move up a row and insert the hook into the center of the stitch above the one just worked. Pull a loop through, then through the loop on the hook.

3. Repeat step 2, being sure to work into the same column of stitches all the way up.

Repeat on the other side.

Mitered Hems

When two hemmed edges meet, for example at the corner of a blanket, a mitered corner makes a neat join. It reduces the bulk of the corners because the two hems don't overlap.

1. Pick up stitches along the edge of the main piece. You can also start with live stitches if you planned ahead and used a provisional cast on. Knit one row to make a fold line.

2. Knit the hem, decreasing one stitch at the mitered edge every right-side row until the hem is the desired depth.

3. Bind off. Fold over and sew the hem edge using either of the techniques for the extended hem.

Mitered hems: The hem on the bottom has been sewn. The hem on the right is ready to be folded and sewn.

Not all yarns or stitches will make clean right angles when the decreases are worked every other row. You can correct for this by decreasing every row occasionally. Use your swatch to determine whether you need to do this, and if so, how frequently to make the adjustment.

Cord Edgings

When you want a simple, neat edge to your knitting, a cord can be the answer. It can be worked along the edge or made separately and sewn in place. Cords can be made in many different ways and don't necessarily involve knitting.

Simple Twisted Cord

Simply twist several strands of yarn together to make a cord. Using different-colored strands will make the cord more decorative.

Simple twisted cord

1. Cut a number of strands of yarn about three times the length of the desired cord. The finished cord will be twice the thickness of the strands, so if you want a cord four strands thick, cut two strands. Knot the strands together at each end.

Knot strands together before twisting.

2. Attach one end to a hook or doorknob or tape it to a table (as shown at right). Twist the strands in your fingers. You can also insert a cable needle through the tied end and, keeping the strands taut, turn the needle clockwise to twist the strands. Don't worry if the strands kink a bit. The tighter the twist, the firmer the cord.

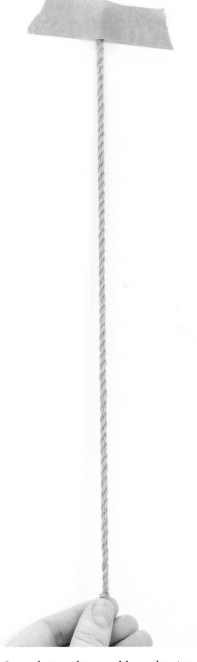

Strands taped to a table and twisted

3. Pinch the twisted strands in the middle and bring the two ends together, allowing the halves of the cord to twist around each other. Tie the ends together and trim them.

Fold twisted strands in half to form the cord.

4. See "Attaching Cord" on page 77 to sew to knitting.

Finger Cord

All you need are your fingers and two balls of yarn to make an easy round cord.

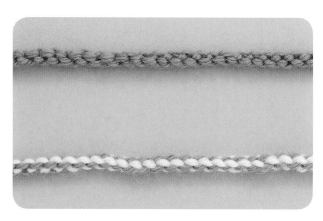

*Finger cords, single color (top)
and two color (bottom)*

1. Tie the two strands together. Hold one strand in each hand and the knot between the left thumb and middle finger. Loop the left strand over the left index finger and hold it next to the knot to create a loop over the finger.

2. Insert the right index finger from front to back into the loop, catch the right strand from underneath, and pull it back through the loop.

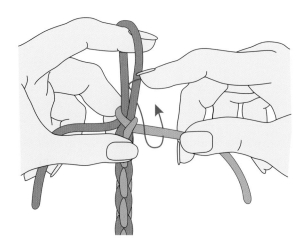

3. Transfer the knot to the right fingers and pull the left strand to tighten the loop. As the cord grows, transfer the cord rather than the knot.

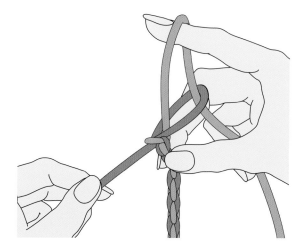

4. Insert the left index finger from front to back into the loop, catch the left strand from underneath, and pull it back through the loop. Take the cord in the left fingers and pull the right strand to tighten the loop.

5. Repeat steps 2–4 until the cord is the desired length. Pull one tail through the loop and tighten.

6. See "Attaching Cord" on page 77 to sew to knitting.

Four-Strand Square Cord

Use this cord for ties, button loops, and frogs, as well as for attaching tassels and pom-poms.

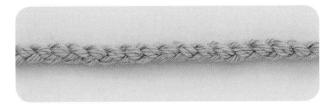

Four-strand square cord

1. Tie four strands, or groups of strands, together at one end. Weight the knotted end on a table, or tape it, so you can gently pull against the strands.

2. Cross the strands and interlace them, with two strands pointing left and two pointing right.

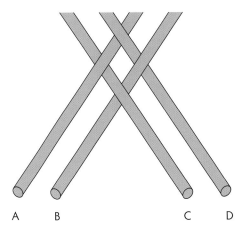

3. Bring the outside left strand (A) around behind the others to the right, then forward between C and D, and drop it next to B. It will be pointing to the left, but will have changed places with B. Gently pull the right and left groups apart to tighten the cord.

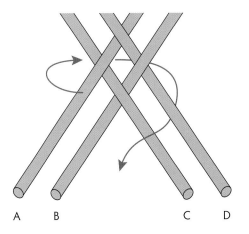

4. Bring the outside right strand (D) around behind the others to the left, then forward between B and A, and drop it next to C. It will be pointing to the right, but will have changed places with C. Gently pull the right and left groups apart to tighten the cord.

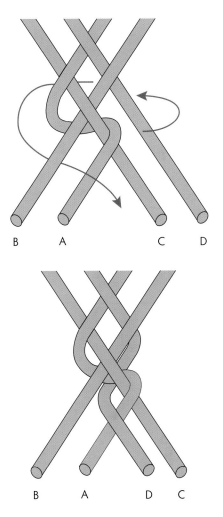

5. Repeat the movements in steps 3 and 4 until the cord is the desired length, bearing in mind that the letters will have changed. Tie a knot.

I-Cord

I-cord makes a neat, rolled edge that gives depth to the edge. I-cord can be made with three to five stitches depending on the thickness you want. You can knit it separately or as part of the edge. In addition, you can use I-cord to make frogs, ties, or drawstrings.

I-cord

1. Using double-pointed needles, cast on three stitches. Do not turn.
2. Slide the stitches to the other end of the needle. Firmly pull the yarn behind the stitches on the needle; then knit them. Do not turn. Repeat this step until the cord is the desired length. Bind off.

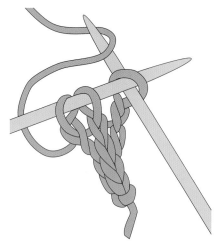

Unattached I-cord

Spiral I-Cord

Spiral I-cord is an unusual-looking decorative cord. Work as for regular I-cord, but alternate knit and purl rows.

Spiral I-cord

Two-Color I-Cord

Use two colors to make a spirally striped I-cord. It takes a little practice to get the tension even.

Two-color I-cord

1. Cast on four stitches with the main color.
2. Work as for regular I-cord, but alternate colors for each stitch, starting with the main color. When switching colors, always bring the contrasting color under the main color.
3. Continue working the I-cord, maintaining the color sequence established on the first row until the cord is the desired length. Bind off.

Striped Two-Color I-Cord

Another version using two colors, this method creates a cord with two stripes on one side. When sewn to an edge, the contrasting-color stripes predominate, making a striking edging.

Two-color I-cord II

1. Cast on five stitches with the main color.
2. Work as for the regular I-cord, alternating colors for each stitch, starting and ending with the main color.
3. Repeat step 2, being careful to bring the main color under the contrasting color at the beginning of each row. Repeat until the cord is the desired length. Bind off.

> ⤙ *Cord Tip* ⤚
>
> Try mixing different colors, textures, or types of yarn to create unique cords.

Attaching Cord

When the cord is finished, no matter how it's made, lay it along the edge of your knitting. Sew it in place with slip stitches (see page 54), hiding the sewing stitches as best you can. If possible, use the same yarn you used to make the cord, as it will blend in and not be noticeable. If it's thick and plied, you may need to separate the plies and use only one or two for sewing. You can also use sewing thread.

A simple twisted cord sewn to edge

Applied I-Cord

Applied I-cord is an easy way to add a neat edge to your work without sewing. As it involves picking up stitches along the edge, you may need to experiment to determine the appropriate ratio for the spacing of the stitches. See "Picking Up Stitches" on page 60.

The I-cord can be worked with any number of stitches required to make the desired thickness of the cord. The examples shown all use three stitches. You can work the applied I-cord by picking up all the stitches first or picking them up as you work the cord.

Applied I-cord

Picking Up Stitches First

1. Pick up and knit stitches along the edge from left to right using a crochet hook. See "Picking Up Stitches along Straight Edges" on page 61.

2. With the right side facing you, cast on three stitches at the end of the left needle using the cable cast on. These are the I-cord stitches.

Cast on three stitches at the end of the left needle after picking up stitches.

3. Knit two I-cord stitches, slip the last cord stitch knitwise, slip the first picked-up stitch knitwise, and knit the two together through the back loop. Slip the cord stitches back to the left needle. Pull the yarn firmly behind the cord stitches. Repeat this step until only the three cord stitches remain on the needle. Bind off.

Picking Up Stitches as Cord Is Worked

You can work this I-cord in two ways: without a yarn over or with a yarn over. I find the yarn over makes the cord neater and I've included it in the following directions. You may find it easier to lift the yarn-over stitch over the stitch with your fingers. Lightly blocking the edge before working the I-cord will help the cord to lie flat on the edge.

1. Cast on three stitches to a double-pointed needle. Do not turn. Slide the stitches to the other end of the needle. These are the I-cord stitches.

2. Knit two I-cord stitches, slip the third stitch purlwise, bring the yarn to the front to make a yarn over, and pick up one stitch along the edge

to which the cord is being attached. Pass the yarn-over stitch over, then the slipped stitch over the first stitch on the right needle and off the needle. Slide the three cord stitches to the other end of the needle and pull the yarn firmly.

3. Repeat step 2 until the I-cord extends across the entire edge. Bind off.

Picking up stitches as the cord is knit

If you need to go around corners with applied I-cord, pick up a stitch at least twice in the corner stitch to prevent the knitting from buckling.

Knit Edging

This is a simple but effective edging that's a bit quicker than knitting I-cord. Pick up and knit stitches along the edge. On the next row, bind off all stitches knitwise.

Knit edging

Pseudo I-Cord

Here's an easy way to make a rolled edge that resembles applied I-cord and can be done on both right and left edges. It shows best on reverse stockinette stitch or a pattern stitch.

Pseudo I-cord shown on the right edge

- **On the right edge of a piece:** On wrong-side rows, work to the last two stitches, bring the yarn to the front, and slip the two stitches purlwise. On right-side rows, knit the first two stitches, pulling the yarn tight on the first stitch.

- **On the left edge of a piece:** On right-side rows, work to the last two stitches, slip the two stitches purlwise with the yarn in back. Turn. On wrong-side rows, purl the first two stitches, pulling the yarn tight on the first stitch.

Crocheted Edgings

Crocheting offers an alternate way of adding decorative edgings. If you don't know how to crochet, it's worth learning to be able to use these finishing techniques.

Crocheted edgings tend to be a little firmer than knitted ones, so they may not be suitable for all projects. If you plan to add crocheted edgings, you may want to use chain-stitch selvage (see page 10) while knitting the project to facilitate the crocheting.

When crocheting an edging, make sure you always insert the hook from front to back under both sides of the edge stitch or the previous crochet stitch. As you work any crocheted edging, you may need to increase or decrease the frequency of stitches picked up through the fabric to keep the edge flat. Experiment to see what works best.

Many crochet stitches can be worked as edgings. Here are a few of the more common ones.

Slip-Stitch Crochet Edge

Often used as a minimal decoration or the base for other crochet stitches, slip-stitch crochet edging produces a very thin edging that won't stop the edge from curling. It can also be used to reinforce seams, especially shoulder and neck seams, to keep them from stretching. It can be worked on either side of your knitted fabric and on any edge.

1. Starting at the right corner, insert the hook into the fabric from front to back and catch the yarn. Pull through a loop, leaving the tail at the back.
2. Insert the hook into the next edge stitch, catch the yarn and pull it through the fabric and the loop on the hook. Repeat this step across the edge. Tie or fasten off.

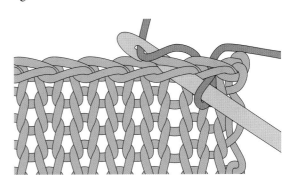

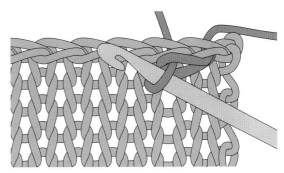

Slip-stitch crochet edging

Single-Crochet Edge

Single crochet produces a more substantial edge that will keep the edge of the knitting from curling if at least two rows are worked. It can be worked on any type of edge. Some like to work this edge with a hook two sizes smaller than the project needles, but don't make the stitches too tight, or the knitted fabric will pucker.

Single-crochet edging

1. With the right side facing you, insert the hook under the edge stitch from front to back, catch the yarn and pull a loop through the fabric. Catch the yarn again and pull it through the loop on the hook.

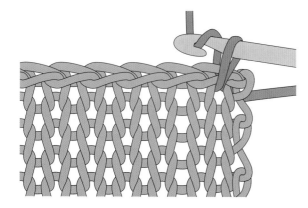

2. Move one or two stitches (or rows) to the left and insert the hook, catch the yarn and pull it through. Catch the yarn again and pull it through

both loops on the hook. Repeat this step across the edge. Fasten off by pulling the tail through the last stitch.

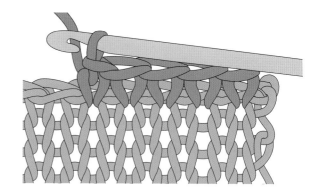

If your edging goes around a corner, work two or three single crochet stitches in the corner hole before turning to work the next edge. The number of stitches in the corner needed to keep the edging flat depends on your yarn thickness and your tension.

For multiple rows of single crochet, work to the end of the edge, turn, and work in the opposite direction, or continue all the way around the edge in the same direction if working on a blanket.

To work in the opposite direction: Turn the work, catch the yarn, and pull it through the loop on the needle (chain one), then work single crochet back, being careful to insert the hook under both sides of the stitches of the previous row.

To continue in same direction: Join the last stitch to the first stitch of the edging with a slip stitch. Chain one and single crochet around again, working under both loops of the stitches of the previous row.

Two rows of single crochet makes a thicker edging. Example shows second row worked in opposite direction from the first row.

Crab Stitch

Also called shrimp stitch, corded edging, and reverse single crochet

Similar to the single-crochet edging, crab stitch is worked from left to right and consists of only one row.

Crab-stitch edging without a base row

1. Starting at the left corner, insert the hook under the edge stitch from front to back, catch the yarn, and pull it through.

2. Insert the hook under the next stitch to the right, catch the yarn as shown, and pull it through the fabric and underneath the loop on the hook.

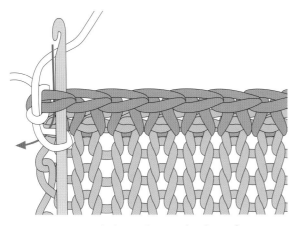

Join yarn with slip stitch. Insert hook into first stitch to the right.

3. Wrap the yarn around the hook as shown, and pull the yarn through both loops on the hook.

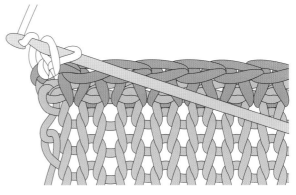

Yarn over hook, pull through both loops on hook.

4. Repeat steps 2 and 3 to the end of the edge.

⟣ Crab-Stitch Options ⟢

To make the edging more visible, you can work a row of single crochet before working the crab stitch. Or try using two strands to make an even more prominent edge.

Slip-Stitch Picot Edge

Inserting a three-chain picot into a knitted slip-stitch selvage makes a decorative edge.

Slip-stitch picot edging

1. Starting at the right corner, insert the hook under the edge stitch from front to back, catch the yarn, and pull it through.

2. Chain three by catching the yarn and pulling it through the loop on the hook three times.

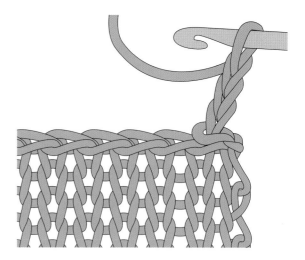

3. Insert the hook into the same edge stitch again, catch the yarn, and pull it through the fabric and the loop on the hook.

4. Insert the hook into the next edge stitch to the left, catch the yarn, and pull it through the fabric and the loop on the hook. Repeat this step once.

5. Repeat steps 2–4 to the end of the edge.

~ Joining a Crocheted Edge ~ in the Round

To prevent a jog when joining the beginning and end of a crocheted edging, try the technique described below. It's similar to preventing a jog in circular knitting (see page 22).

Insert the hook where you want to start the edging and pull a loop through. This is the beginning loop. Then work a single crochet chain in the next stitch and continue around. After working the last stitch back at the beginning, cut the yarn, leaving a long tail, and pull the end through the two loops on the hook. Thread the end on a yarn needle. Insert the needle under both sides of the beginning loop, then into the center of the last single crochet chain. Pull the yarn so the tension of this last stitch matches that of the edging and tie off.

Buttons and Buttonholes

Buttons are the most common method for closing knitted garments. Ideally, purchase your buttons before starting your project so you'll know exactly how big your buttonholes need to be.

BUTTONS

Buttons with shanks are well suited for knitted garments. The shank keeps the button from being too tight, which would cause the band to pucker. The length of the shank should be about the same thickness as the knitted band.

Shank buttons come in all sizes and shapes.

When sewing on buttons, you can use sewing thread or your project yarn. I find that thread makes a stronger attachment, but it isn't always possible to find the same color as your yarn. If the exact shade isn't available, use a slightly darker color. The color won't be a problem if you use your project yarn, but not all buttons have holes large enough to accommodate the thickness of yarn. If your yarn is plied, you can always separate the plies and use just two of them for sewing.

Sewing Shank Buttons

Overlap the buttonhole and button bands so the buttonhole band is on top. Insert a removable marker through the buttonhole and fasten it to the button band to mark the position of each button. Sew the buttons to the band.

Marking the button placement on the button band

Sewing Flat Buttons

Flat buttons can also be used on knitted garments, although they may not be suitable for all knitted fabrics. If the fabric isn't too thick, you may be able to sew the buttons as you would onto any fabric. The button will go completely through the buttonhole without causing the band to pucker.

For thicker fabrics, make a thread shank for the button to accommodate the fabric thickness. Simply add a spacer to elongate the threads attaching the button. A thin pencil, double-pointed needle about the same size as your project needles, or something of equivalent thickness works well.

1. Place the spacer on top of the fabric and place the button on top of it. Then sew the button on as you normally would.

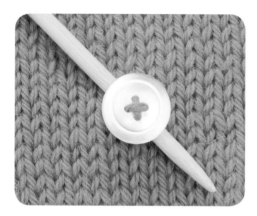

Use a double-pointed needle below the button as a spacer.

2. Bring the yarn to the right side, remove the spacer, pull up on the button, and wind the yarn around the thread attaching the button to form a shank. Then tie off.

Wrap yarn around the threads to form a shank.

If your knitted fabric is loose and lacking body, place a small, flat button on the wrong side and sew the two buttons together on either side of the band.

Sew a flat button to the wrong side of the band to reinforce the button on the right side.

Knit Buttons

If you can't find the right button for your project, you can knit your own. Using the project yarn guarantees the color will match! Knit buttons can also be a nice design element and make the entire garment completely handmade.

The number of stitches and rows depends on your yarn and gauge. Experiment to see what works best for your yarn and gives you the right size button. If your yarn is fine, using a double strand of yarn will help make the button full and firm.

Knit button

1. Cast on five stitches. Work in stockinette stitch for about six or seven rows, ending with a knit row.

2. Slip the second, third, fourth, and fifth stitches individually over the first stitch and off the needle. Break the yarn leaving about a 9" or 10" tail and pull the tail through the loop.

3. Thread the tail onto a yarn needle and sew a running stitch around the edge. Pull the tail to shape the button, tie the two tails together, and use them to attach the button.

Sew a running stitch around the button. White yarn was used for clarity.

⊸ *Choosing Buttons* ⊸

Buttons can blend in with the knitting or provide a striking contrast. When choosing buttons, keep the weight of the yarn and thickness of the knitted fabric in mind. Small buttons will be lost on thick fabric, slip through the buttonholes, and not keep the garment closed. Heavy buttons on lighter fabrics will weigh down the band, pulling it out of shape.

BUTTONHOLES

Buttonholes are an important part of finishing a garment. When poorly done, they can detract from an otherwise beautifully made sweater. When worked well, they shouldn't require any further finishing. They're often used in a ribbed band, but they work equally well in garter-stitch, seed-stitch, or stockinette-stitch bands.

Buttonholes should fit into the band without disturbing the pattern stitch. The size of a buttonhole depends on your yarn as well as on the size of the button. Some yarns are stretchier than others. Buttonholes can stretch to almost twice their original size, so it's better to make them slightly smaller than the button. Nothing is more annoying than a button that doesn't stay in its hole. When unsure how big to make a buttonhole, use your swatch to determine the appropriate number of rows or stitches. See "Swatches" on page 8.

Buttonholes are usually placed on bands that are knit either as part of the garment or added afterward. They should be placed about ½" from both the top and bottom edges of the band. The remaining buttons can then be placed where you want them. They can be evenly spaced along the band or grouped to make a design statement.

It's most common for buttons and buttonholes to be centered in the width of the button band. A button, however, doesn't stay in the center of a horizontal buttonhole. With movement, it will be pulled to the outer corner of the buttonhole. If it's important for the buttons to be exactly in line, you may want to place them a little off center.

There are many ways to work buttonholes. Here are several. Try them all to see which work best for you.

⊸ *Placing Buttons Evenly* ⊸

I usually measure the distance between the top and bottom buttons, divide that by the number of buttons, and then place the buttons. For most cardigans I keep the distance between buttons to 3" or less. If the band is garter stitch, I measure and then double-check to make sure there are the same number of ridges between buttons. Sometimes you need to fiddle a bit, in which case I usually place the top two buttons slightly closer together. Not for any logical reason, though. I just do it.

Eyelet Buttonhole

Also called yarn-over buttonhole

The simplest buttonhole to work, the eyelet buttonhole creates a small, round hole. But thanks to the elasticity of the knitted fabric, it can be suitable for surprisingly larger buttons than you might think.

Eyelet buttonhole

1. On the right side, work to where you want the buttonhole, bring the yarn to the front to make a yarn over, knit two stitches together, and work to end.
2. On the next row, work the yarn over as a stitch.

With K1, P1 ribbing, the eyelet buttonhole is less obtrusive if it's worked over a purl stitch.

1. Work to the purl stitch, make a yarn over, knit two stitches together (the purl stitch and the knit stitch to its left).
2. On the next row, work the yarn over as a stitch, keeping in the rib pattern.

Eyelet buttonhole in ribbing

Reinforced Eyelet Buttonhole

A reinforced eyelet produces a strong, neat buttonhole.

Reinforced eyelet buttonhole

1. On the right side, work to where you want the buttonhole, bring the yarn to the front to make a yarn over, work to the end.
2. On the next row, work to the yarn over and slip it purlwise, wrap the yarn around the needle to make another yarn over, work to the end.
3. On the next row (right side), work to the stitch before the yarn overs, slip one stitch as if to knit, knit the yarn overs together, but do not drop them from the needle, pass the slipped stitch over the stitch just made, knit three stitches together (the yarn overs and next stitch), and work to the end.

Knit the two yarn overs together to make a reinforced eyelet buttonhole.

Large Eyelet Buttonhole

Also called three-row buttonhole

Large eyelet buttonhole

1. On the right side, work to where you want the buttonhole, bring the yarn to the front to make a yarn over, then wrap the yarn around the needle again to make a second yarn over, knit two stitches together through the back loop, work to the end.
2. On the next row, work to the yarn overs, purl the first, drop the second, and work to the end.
3. On the next row (right side), work to the worked yarn over, knit into the hole below the yarn over, drop the worked yarn-over stitch, and work to the end.

Knitting into the hole below the yarn over

Vertical Buttonhole

The vertical buttonhole is a continuation of the large eyelet buttonhole, but the result is oblong rather than round.

Vertical buttonhole

1. Work steps 1–3 of the large eyelet buttonhole (at left).
2. On the next row (wrong side), work to the buttonhole, purl into the buttonhole, drop the next stitch, and work to the end.

Buttonhole Variety

Buttonholes can be small or large, round, vertical, or horizontal. They can be knit or crocheted, worked as you knit the garment, or added as an afterthought. No matter how they're made, there's a perfect buttonhole for every project.

Horizontal Buttonhole

Also called single buttonhole, cast-on buttonhole, simple horizontal buttonhole, standard buttonhole, two-row buttonhole

Probably the most commonly used buttonhole, a horizontal buttonhole is worked over two rows. The number of stitches bound off depends on the diameter (width) of your button.

Horizontal buttonhole

1. On the right side, work to where you want the buttonhole, bind off the required number of stitches, and work to the end.

Bound-off stitches form the buttonhole.

2. On the next row, work to the bound-off stitches, turn the work and cast on the same number of stitches that were bound off using the cable cast-on method. Before slipping the last stitch to the left needle, bring the yarn forward so that it's between the last two stitches. Turn and work to the end.

While the cable cast on is most commonly used with this buttonhole, the buttonhole cast on (see page 92) works extremely well, but it can be a little tricky to get the right tension.

One-Row Buttonhole

For smoother edges on a horizontal buttonhole, try this variation. It produces a strong, neat hole with reinforced sides, making it less elastic than other buttonholes. Although the photo below shows the buttonhole on a stockinette-stitch fabric, the buttonhole is less obtrusive when worked on garter stitch and reverse stockinette stitch.

One-row buttonhole

1. On the right side, work to where you want the buttonhole. With the yarn forward, slip one stitch as if to purl, then bring yarn to the back.
2. Slip one stitch purlwise, then pass the first slipped stitch over the second as though to bind off.
3. Repeat step 2 until the desired number of stitches is bound off; slip the last stitch back to left needle.

Bind off stitches to form the buttonhole.

4. Turn and bring the yarn to the back. Using the cable cast-on method, cast on the same number of stitches as you bound off plus one. Bring the yarn to the front before slipping the last stitch to the left needle so it's between the last two stitches.
5. Turn, slip one stitch knitwise, and pass the extra cast-on stitch over. Work to the end.

Reinforced Horizontal Buttonhole

This is a stronger version of the horizontal buttonhole. Although it works best with the buttonhole cast on (see page 92), you may find it easier to use the knit or cable cast on. Those cast ons require turning your work for the cast on, and they don't create as neat a hole as the buttonhole cast on.

Reinforced horizontal buttonhole

1. On the right side, work to where you want the buttonhole, knit into the back of the stitch below the first stitch on the left needle, then knit the stitch on the needle.

Knit through the top of the stitch below the next stitch on the left needle.

2. Knit one stitch, pass the previous stitch over as though to bind off.

3. Repeat step 2 for all stitches to be bound off except one stitch.

4. Knit into the back of the stitch below the first stitch on the left needle, then knit the stitch on the needle, pass the third stitch on the right needle over the two stitches just made, and work to the end.

Passing the previous stitch over

5. On the next row, work to two stitches before the buttonhole, purl two stitches together, cast on the same number of stitches bound off plus two more stitches, purl two stitches together, and work to the end.

6. On the next row, work to the stitch before the buttonhole, slip the next two stitches knitwise (the side stitch and the first cast-on stitch), then knit them together through the back loops, work to the last cast-on stitch, knit two stitches together (last cast-on stitch and side stitch), and work to end.

Forgotten Buttonhole

If you forget to make buttonholes or decide to add them as an afterthought, use this clever way to make a vertical buttonhole in knit one, purl one ribbing. This buttonhole is relatively small but not as elastic as some.

Forgotten buttonhole

1. With the wrong side facing you, insert a crochet hook into a purl stitch in the middle of where you want the buttonhole.

2. Catch the top of the purl stitch above the stitch and pull it down under the first purl stitch and through. Then catch the top of the next stitch and pull it through the loop on the hook.

Pull the top of the purl stitch through the purl stitch below.

3. Pull up on the loop on the hook and thread a piece of yarn through it. Pull the yarn to open the hole and tie it off.

Thread yarn through the loop. A contrasting color was used for clarity.

4. Rotate the piece and repeat steps 1–3 at the bottom of the buttonhole.

⚊ Buttonholes with ⚊ Slippery Yarns

If your yarn is very slippery, try this trick to make a slightly firmer buttonhole. Add a strand or two of matching sewing thread as you knit the buttonhole. Add the thread on the row immediately before the buttonhole and drop it when the buttonhole is finished.

Crocheted Buttonhole

Slits can be incorporated into a crocheted edging to make firm, vertical buttonholes. Use a hook about two sizes smaller than your project needle.

Crocheted buttonhole

1. Work several rows of single-crochet edging along the knitted edge until the edging is half the width of the desired final band.

➤ Avoiding the Gape ➤

Do you hate a gaping button band on the front of a cardigan? You can avoid this by carefully placing the buttonholes. Set the first buttonhole at the widest point of the bust or chest. Then evenly space the remaining buttonholes.

---

2. Crochet another row, stopping at the point where you want the buttonhole. Make a chain the length of the buttonhole. Skip that same length on the edge, then resume inserting the hook into the edge. Repeat for each buttonhole, taking care to chain the same number of stitches for each buttonhole.

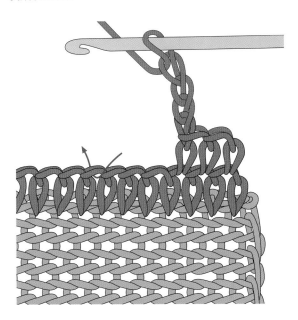

3. On the next row, single crochet to the chain stitches, work the same number of single crochet stitches into the hole as there are in the chain. Repeat for each buttonhole to end.

4. Finish the band.

Buttonhole Cast On

Use this cast on when you need to add stitches in the middle of your work.

1. With the right side facing you, and the needle in your right hand, hold the yarn taut in the left hand. *Swing the left thumb behind and under the strand, and then up to wrap the yarn around the thumb. Insert the needle into the thumb loop as if to knit.

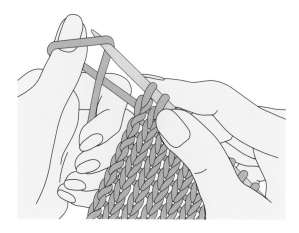

2. Wrap the yarn around the needle tip as if to knit, and lift the thumb loop up and over the needle tip and off the needle.

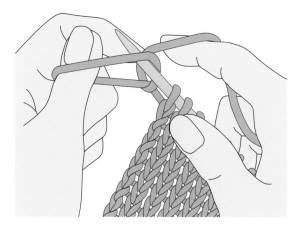

3. Place the left thumb on top of the stitch to keep it in position, and then tighten the stitch by pulling the yarn with the right-hand fingers. Repeat from * for required number of stitches.

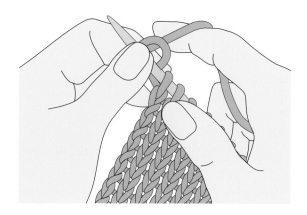

BUTTON LOOPS

Many closures can be made after you've finished knitting, so they're well suited when buttons are an afterthought.

Sewn Loops

Simple yarn loops can be added to any edge.

Sewn loop

1. Thread a piece of yarn on a yarn needle. Insert the needle through the edge from back to front at one end of the loop, then through the edge from front to back at the other end. Then insert the needle from back to front through the first hole again, resulting in a double loop on the edge.

Make a double loop on the edge.

2. Use a yarn needle and the tail to work buttonhole stitches tightly over the double loops and the short yarn end. (Needle under the double loops and over the working yarn; pull snug.) Secure the end and trim.

Work buttonhole stitches over the loop.

Crocheted Loops

Made with a single strand of project yarn, a crocheted loop is an easy way to make a neat, thin loop.

1. Leaving long tails at either end, crochet a single chain long enough to fit snugly around the button. If your yarn is very elastic, you might want to make the chain slightly shorter.

2. Use a yarn needle to attach both ends of the chain to the wrong side of the edge. Make sure the ends are securely attached so the loop can't stretch.

Sew crocheted chain loop to the wrong side of the edge.

Alternately, you can crochet the ends of the chain directly to the fabric edge. Adding a row of single crochet along the chain loop creates an attractive edge that is stronger than the single chain.

1. With the wrong side facing you, insert the hook into the edge at the upper end of the buttonhole from back to front and pull through a loop, leaving a tail long enough to weave in. Crochet a chain long enough to fit around the button.

2. Insert the hook into the edge where you want the button loop to end, catch the yarn, and pull a loop through the fabric and the loop on the hook.

Attach the crocheted chain loop directly to the edge with a hook.

3. Chain one, turn and work a single crochet along the loop to the other end, and fasten off.

Work single crochet along the crocheted loop.

I-Cord Loops

I-cord provides an alternate means of making loops. Due to the nature of I-cord, the loops will be thicker than crocheted ones.

Simple I-Cord Loops

The simplest way to make a loop is to knit a two- or three-stitch I-cord. The number of stitches will depend on how thick you want the loops to be. Make the I-cord long enough to fit snugly around the button. Use the tails at both ends of the cord to sew the loop to the wrong side of the edge.

Simple I-cord loop

Applied I-Cord Loops

You can also work buttonholes in an applied I-cord edging. One way is to work the applied I-cord up to where you want the buttonhole, work a few rows of I-cord without attaching it to the edge, and then resume attaching the I-cord, keeping the I-cord taut along the edge. The number of unattached rows will depend on the diameter of the button.

Buttonhole slit in I-cord edging

Similarly, you can make a loop in an applied I-cord edge. When you reach the point where you want the loop, stop attaching the I-cord and make an unattached section; it should be long enough to form a loop large enough for the button. Then resume attaching the I-cord at the point where you left off before making the loop.

Loop made as part of applied I-cord

⟶ Details Are Important ⟵

Buttonholes and loops are finishing details that may seem unimportant, but that's far from true. A sloppy one can ruin an otherwise beautifully made garment. If worked with care, none of the button closures described in this chapter should require further stitching.

Frogs

Frogs are fancy closures made from I-cord loops and can add an elegant touch to your garment. You can be creative in designing frogs to make them as simple or elaborate as you wish. Knit buttons work well with knit frogs. See "Knit Buttons" on page 84.

I-cord frog and knit button

Plan the design of the frog, making at least one loop for the buttonhole. Then make the I-cord as thick or thin as you want and as long as needed to make your design. Pin the frog in place and sew it to the fabric with the same yarn you used to make the frog. If your yarn is plied, you may find it easier to sew using only one or two plies.

Zippers

Putting zippers in knitted garments may seem daunting. Although they can be a bit fussy, they are actually relatively easy to sew in and make a good alternative to buttons. Take time to work the steps with care and you'll have excellent results.

There are two kinds of zippers: separating and closed bottom. Separating zippers, as their name suggests, consist of two pieces that zip together. They're ideal for cardigans and other projects that will open all the way. Closed-bottom zippers are used for partial openings, for example on pullover neck openings.

Zippers come in several standard sizes. Measure the length of the opening and try to buy a zipper the same length. If you can't find one the right length, you have two options. If the difference is ½" or less, you can use a shorter one. The top edge of the knitting can extend a little bit above the top of the zipper without looking funny.

If the difference is greater than ½", buy a longer zipper and cut it to the right size. To do this, measure the desired length on the zipper. At the lower point, whipstitch across the zipper coil 8 or 10 times using a double strand of sewing thread. You can also stitch across the coil using a machine. Then cut the zipper about ½" below the stitching.

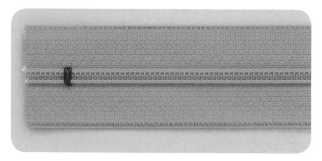

To shorten a zipper, whipstitch across the coil and then trim the zipper end.

Edgings with Zippers

Choose an appropriate edge (selvage) stitch to make putting in the zipper easier and help maintain a neat edge. Two-stitch selvages, such as the two-stitch garter-stitch selvage (see page 11) or a row of single crochet (see page 80), work well with zippers because they firm up the edge. The pseudo I-cord (see page 78) and the knit edging (see page 78) are two other suitable options.

⟿ Simple Two-Row Reverse ⟿ Stockinette-Stitch Edging

Here's another simple edging that works well with zippers.

Two-row reverse stockinette-stitch edging for a zipper opening

1. With the right side facing you, pick up stitches along the edge.
2. Turn and knit one row; then bind off purling.

Sewing in a Zipper

Preshrink the zipper by washing it as you will the finished garment. This is an important step, as the cotton tapes will shrink with repeated washings and pull the edge out of shape. Washing will also flatten the tape, getting rid of the creases from being folded in the package.

1. Lightly block the knitted edges to make positioning the zipper easier.
2. With the right side of the garment facing you, place the closed zipper along the edges of the opening and pin it in place. Make sure it's also right side up! Take extra care to make sure the positioning is correct, and don't be stingy with pins. Align the bottom of the zipper flush with the bottom edges of the garment.

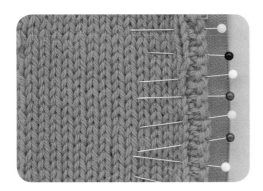

Closed zipper pinned to one side

Remember that knitting is stretchy and zippers are not. When placing the zipper, make very sure that you don't stretch the knitting to fit the zipper. If you do, the zipper and the knitting will not lie flat.

Make sure the edges of the fabric meet in the middle of the teeth and cover the teeth. Some knitters recommend placing the edges against the outer edges of the teeth to keep the fabric from catching in the teeth. I find that no matter how much the edges cover the teeth at this stage, by the end of the sewing process the edges have moved slightly away from each other to the extent that they won't impede the movement of the zipper. If you leave too large a gap at the beginning, the tape will show, which is not very attractive.

3. At the top of the zipper, fold the excess edges of the tape back on themselves and away from the zipper so they're out of the way.

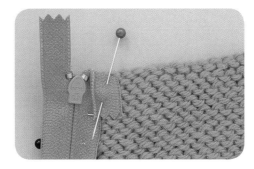

Fold the top edge of the tape out of the way.

4. With the wrong side facing you, baste the zipper in place. Remove the pins.
5. With the right side facing you, hand sew the zipper in place using neat, even backstitches. Work the stitches one at a time, inserting the needle straight down to prevent the thread from pulling the zipper band. If possible, stitch along the ditch between a column of stitches to help keep the sewing straight and less visible.

Sew the zipper in place. Blue stitches are the basting stitches from step 4.

6. Using the whipstitch, tack the edges of the tape to the fabric on the wrong side.

Tack down the edges of the tape.

Pockets

Pockets can be made in many different ways, most of which are part of the knitting process. The ones presented here are added as part of the finishing process with the exception of the inset pocket. It's included here because it involves additional work to complete it.

Patch Pockets

Patch pockets are knit separately and sewn to the garment during finishing. They can be part of your original design or added as an afterthought. A stockinette-stitch or chain-stitch selvage on the pocket will greatly facilitate sewing. See "Selvage Stitches" on page 9.

Patch pocket

It's best to sew patch pockets onto a flat piece before the final assembly of the garment. This makes it easier to keep both pieces flat and keep the pocket from moving during sewing, resulting in better placement of the pocket and neater, straighter seams.

1. Block both pieces. Carefully position the pocket, following rows in the fabric on the top and bottom of the pocket and columns of fabric stitches on the sides. Pin the pocket in place. With a contrasting-color yarn, baste around the edge of the pocket one stitch away from the edge of the pocket and as straight as possible to serve as a guide for sewing.

White basting stitches mark the position of the pocket.

2. Stitch the pocket along the edge. You can use the slip stitch (see page 54), but I find the mattress stitch makes a neater edge. Use the mattress stitch for selvage to selvage (see page 43) along the sides and the mattress stitch for bound-off edges (see page 45) along the bottom. Be careful to match the pocket and fabric row for row for even pocket edges. Take care to sew the top corners of the pocket firmly as they will take considerable stress and wear.

Picked-Up Pockets

You can avoid the bottom seam on a pocket by picking up stitches along the fabric using a knitting needle and a crochet hook. This makes a neater and tighter bottom edge to the pocket.

Picked-up pocket

1. Determine where you want the pocket to be. Using different-color yarn, mark the row below the bottom of the pocket and also where the two lower corners will be. You want to pick up stitches along a single row at the bottom of the pocket.
2. Starting at the lower-right corner, follow directions for picking up stitches in the middle of work (see page 63) to pick up the stitches for the pocket.

Pick up stitches using the basting stitches as a guide.

3. Attach a new strand and work the pocket with seams or by attaching the pocket sides as described at right.

Pocket Worked with Seams

On the first (wrong-side) row, increase one stitch at both the beginning and end of the row. These two stitches are selvage stitches and will be incorporated into the pocket seam. Keep these stitches in stockinette stitch as you work the pocket to the required length and bind off.

Use the mattress stitch for selvage to selvage (see page 43) to sew the side seams to the fabric as you would a patch pocket.

Pocket Worked without Seams

1. Attach a new strand and work the first (wrong-side) row of the pocket.
2. On the next row, with the yarn in back, skip the stitch on the fabric immediately above the first pocket stitch and pick up the left side of the stitch above it (two stitches above the first pocket stitch), place it on the left needle, and knit it together with the first pocket stitch.

Pick up stitches along the right side of the pocket.

3. Work to the last stitch and slip it to the right needle knitwise. With the left needle, pick up the right leg of the stitch on the fabric above the last pocket stitch. Slip the last stitch on the right needle onto the left needle and knit the two stitches together through the back loop. Turn and work back.

Pick up stitches along the left side of the pocket.

4. Repeat steps 1 and 2. When the pocket is the right height, bind off.

Inset Pockets

Inset pockets are worked as you knit your garment. The pocket lining is knit separately and is then joined to the body at the top of the pocket. After the knitting is finished, the lining is sewn to the wrong side of the garment.

Block the lining and pin it in place on the wrong side of the garment. Use the slip stitch (see page 54) or one of the variations of the mattress stitch (see page 42) to sew the lining edge to the wrong side of the garment. Be careful to keep the stitches small so they don't show on the front. Also, don't pull the stitches too tight or the seam will show on the right side.

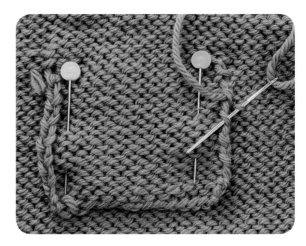

Sew the inset pocket lining to the wrong side of the garment.

Added Touches

Embellishments are a fun and creative way to add flair to your knitting. Entire books have been devoted to the many options. How about adding fringes, tassels, or pom-poms? Here are three common methods to get you started.

Fringes

Fringes are commonly used for edgings on knitting, especially on scarves, blankets, and afghans. The number of strands in each fringe will depend on your yarn and in turn will determine the thickness of the fringe as well as the spacing of the fringe. They should be evenly spaced.

Fringe along an edge

1. Cut yarn into strands of the same length, a little more than twice the length you want the final fringe to be.

Fringes can be knotted to create a lacy edging.

2. Fold strands (one, two, or more) in half and pull the folded end through the knitting's edge to the back with a hook. Then pull the ends through the loop and pull on them to tighten the knot. Once all the fringes are in place, trim them so they are even.

Fold the fringe and pull the center of the strands through the loop with a crochet hook.

Tassels

Tassels are often used to finish a hat, either on the crown or on the end of ties. They can also be added to the corners of pillows or the end of a cord.

Tassels

1. Cut a piece of cardboard slightly taller than the desired length of the tassel. Wrap the yarn around the cardboard. The more wraps, the fuller the tassel.

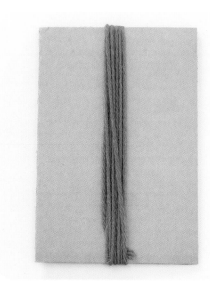

Wrap yarn around a piece of cardboard.

2. Cut a length of yarn, thread it under the wrapped strands at one edge of the cardboard, and tie the two ends together to gather the wraps. Leave long ends.

Thread yarn under the strands to tie them together.

3. Cut the strands along the edge of the cardboard that's opposite the knot.

Cut the strands.

4. Wrap another strand several times tightly around the tassel below the tied end. Tie the ends together, thread them onto a needle, and work them through the top of the tassel. Trim the ends.

Tie a strand around the top of the tassel to form a head.

⟣ *Using Tassels* ⟣

Tassels don't need to be limited to pillows or cords. Try adding them as accents to ponchos, hoods, capes, or earflap hats.

Pom-Poms

Pom-poms are often used to decorate hats, but can be added to any knitted piece. They can be made in a single color or with many colors, depending on your fancy.

The directions here are for a cardboard template. However, if you make many pom-poms, you may want to buy a plastic template, which is available at most yarn and craft stores.

Pom-poms

1. Cut two cardboard circles, each with a diameter slightly larger than the desired width of the pom-pom. Cut a center hole and a small wedge out of each circle.

Cardboard circle for making a pom-pom

2. Holding the two cardboard circles together, wrap yarn tightly around the arc. The more wraps, the fuller the pom-pom will be.

Wrap yarn around cardboard circles.

3. Cut the yarn by carefully slipping scissors between the two pieces of cardboard.

Cut the yarn with scissors.

4. Carefully pull the two cardboard circles apart slightly and slip a piece of yarn between them. Tie the ends tightly in a secure knot and remove the cardboard.

Wrap a strand of yarn around the center of the pom-pom between cardboard circles.

5. Gently pull the yarn ends to cover the central knot. Fluff out the pom-pom and trim the edges to make it smooth and round.

Washing

It isn't always necessary to wash knitting after you finish your piece. It will freshen up the piece, however, especially if it has gotten dirty during knitting. Sometimes washing can be used instead of blocking.

When washing, follow the directions on the yarn band. Many yarn manufacturers now place International Textile Care Labeling Code symbols (page 106) on their yarn bands. These can be helpful guides. If you're unsure about how to wash your piece, wash your swatch to see what works best.

Avoid using harsh detergents. They can alter the feel of your knitting and permanently damage the surface of some fibers. Dishwashing liquids work well as long as they don't contain strong dyes. Choose one that is clear or white. Shampoo can also be used if it's clear or white.

In addition, there are several products specifically designed for washing handknits, especially wool. They contain lanolin, so they will soften not just wool, but all animal fibers. They're not advisable for use with cottons and silks as they may leave residues.

When washing knitting, it's important to remember that all protein fibers (including wool, alpaca, llama, cashmere, and silk) are more fragile when wet. Unless handled with care, wet garments made from these fibers can be permanently stretched out of shape. This is not the case with cotton and linen, which become stronger when wet. Even so, it's best to handle all wet knitting carefully.

Colorfastness

Before washing any knitting, it's wise to test a piece of yarn to make sure it's colorfast, especially if your piece has several colors. You don't want one to bleed into the others. In many yarns, the dye is actually fast. What you see bleeding out is excess dye. Once that has been washed out, your piece should be colorfast. If you know that there is excess dye in your yarn, you might want to wash it before you begin knitting. If your yarn is in a hank, carefully undo the hank and wash it gently in a large bowl until the water runs clear. Lay flat to dry. If your yarn is in a ball, wind it onto a yarn winder to make a hank. Then wash and dry.

Test your yarn. See "Blocking" on page 24. If it does bleed, you can set the dye with a rinse prior to washing. Add ¼ cup of vinegar to a gallon of water and use it to rinse your piece. Don't soak it in the vinegar water, just rinse it.

Hand Washing

Good hand washing can extend the life of your knitting. It is the gentlest cleaning method and the one that gives you the greatest control. All natural fibers are best washed by hand regardless of what the label says.

Fill a basin or sink with lukewarm water (86°F/30°C). Add a mild soap or detergent and swish it around in the water to distribute it evenly. Then immerse your piece and hold it down to get rid of the air bubbles and saturate the fibers. Gently squeeze the soap through the knitting. Be very careful not to rub the knitting, especially wool, as this could felt it.

Allow the knitting to soak 10 to 15 minutes, then drain the water. Gently squeeze the knitting to remove as much water as possible. Fill the basin again with clean, lukewarm water and gently swish the knitting around to remove the soap. Drain the basin again and repeat until the rinse water is clean and the knitting doesn't feel soapy.

If, after several rinses, you still feel soap in the knitting, add a few tablespoons of vinegar to the next rinse. This helps break down the soap and allow it to be rinsed away. Give the knitting a final rinse.

After the final rinse, gently squeeze the knitting to remove as much water as possible. Never wring or twist wet knitting. Twisting can permanently stretch and damage the fibers. Roll the knitting up in a large towel and squeeze to draw out more water as you would for immersion blocking. See "Immersion" on page 28. You can also remove water by placing the knitting in your washing machine set to the spin cycle. Carefully spread out the knitting evenly in the bottom of the drum so the machine won't be off balance and spin for 10 to 15 seconds only.

Washing

⊠	Do not wash
⊔	Hand wash in warm water
30°	Hand wash at stated temperature
▣ ▣	Machine wash
⊠	Do not tumble dry
▢	Tumble drying OK
⊟	Dry flat
⊠	No bleach
△	Chlorine bleach OK

Pressing

⊠	Do not iron
⌒	Cool iron
⌒	Warm iron
⌒	Hot iron

Dry Cleaning

⊗	Do not dry clean
Ⓐ	Dry cleanable in all solvents
Ⓕ	Dry cleanable with fluorocarbon or petroleum-based solvents only
Ⓟ	Dry cleanable with perchlorethylene, hydrocarbons, or a petroleum-based solvent

Machine Washing

Some yarns, especially superwash yarns, can be washed in a machine. Generally, the gentlest cycle is best. Use the water temperature indicated on the yarn label. If there isn't a recommendation, it's wise to use cold water. As with hand washing, use a mild soap or detergent. Remove your knitting as soon as the cycle is finished and lay it out flat as for hand washing. Bear in mind, though, that superwash wool will eventually shrink and mat with many washings.

It's always a good idea to turn garments inside out before washing them in a machine. This protects the right side from excessive agitation. To further protect garments from stretching, place them in a mesh bag before putting them in the machine. If you can't find a mesh bag large enough, a pillowcase knotted or tied works well.

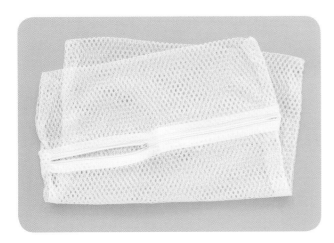

Mesh laundry bag

Cottons can be successfully machine washed and dried, but after many successive washings, they will shrink and can lose their softness. Sometimes this shrinking can be an advantage. Because cotton garments, especially socks, can stretch during wearing, machine washing can help to shrink them back to size. To prolong the life of cotton garments, alternate between hand and machine washing.

Drying

It's almost always best to dry knitted pieces flat. Spread your piece out on a clean, flat surface as you would for blocking. See "Laying Out" on page 26. You can use a bath towel or a mesh rack designed specifically for this purpose. The latter works well because both sides are exposed to air and your piece will dry faster. I use my patio table as its surface is rigid, but the open holes in the tabletop allow good ventilation.

Gently spread out the knitting to the correct dimensions. Don't pull your piece, which can stretch it. Gently pick it up and move it in small increments until it is in the right position. Ease out any wrinkles with your hands. Line up edges on garments. Allow the piece to dry completely before moving it.

Dry cottons in a dryer on a low or delicate setting. Remove them when they're almost dry and lay them flat to finish drying.

Acknowledgments

Many people helped bring this book into being and I am extremely grateful to them all. My thanks go to:

Everyone at Martingale, especially content director Karen Soltys and technical editor Ursula Reikes. Their patience, thoughtfulness, and skill make them a joy to work with and are responsible for turning one's work into a beautiful book.

Patti Garland, for reading the entire manuscript. Her comments and suggestions have made this a much better book than it would have been otherwise.

Lorilee Beltman and Peggy Skiles, for helping to knit swatches. Even though some got lost in the mail, I appreciate the effort!

Cascade Yarn, for generously providing all the yarn used in this book.

And to David, for providing support and encouragement all along the way.

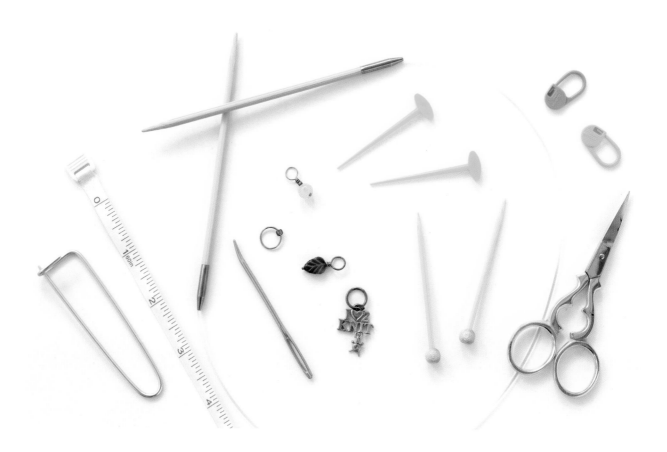

About the Author

Photo ©Gale Zucker/www.gzucker.com

Avid knitter Cap Sease has been knitting since childhood, having learned from her grandmother. She is also a weaver, quilter, and basket maker. Her love of using her hands led to a career in art conservation, working with archaeological and ethnographic objects.

She has worked primarily in museums, but she also has extensive experience as a conservator on archaeological excavations in the Mediterranean and Middle East. Since 2005 Cap has been a designer for the Green Mountain Spinnery and has taught workshops on various techniques, including cast ons and bind offs, for their Knitters' Weekends. The author of the best-selling *Cast On, Bind Off* (Martingale, 2012), Cap lives in Connecticut with her husband, David.

Index